MW00856539

BATTLE FOR THE SOUTHERN FRONTIER

THE CREEK WAR AND THE WAR OF 1812

MIKE BUNN & CLAY WILLIAMS

Charleston H London
THE
History
PRESS

Published by The History Press
Charleston, SC 29403
www.historypress.net

Cover image: "The Georgia Militia under General Floyd attacking the Creek Indians at Autossee." *Courtesy of the Hargrett Rare Book and Manuscript Library/University of Georgia Libraries.*

First published 2008
Second printing 2012
Third printing 2012
Fourth printing 2013

Manufactured in the United States

ISBN 978.1.59629.371.7

Library of Congress Cataloging-in-Publication Data
Bunn, Mike.
Battle for the southern frontier : the Creek War and the War of 1812 / Mike Bunn and
Clay Williams.
p. cm.
Includes bibliographical references.
ISBN 978-1-59629-371-7
1. Creek War, 1813-1814--Campaigns. 2. Southern States--History--War of
1812--Campaigns. 3. United States--History--War of 1812--Campaigns. 4. Gulf
States--History, Military--19th century. I. Williams, Clay, 1970- II. Title.
E83.813.B86 2008
973.5'238--dc22
2008019746

This book is dedicated to those historians who informed and inspired our work: Henry Sale Halbert and Timothy Horton Ball, whose pioneering work still serves as the foundation for any study of the Creek War; Frank Lawrence Owsley Jr., whose landmark study documented the link between the Creek War and the larger War of 1812 and remains a standard reference source for understanding this chapter in Gulf South history; and Robert Remini, the foremost scholar on the life of Andrew Jackson and one of the leading authorities on the Battle of New Orleans.

As these scholars have demonstrated, the Creek War and the War of 1812 were cataclysmic turning points in American history, replete with heroes and legendary figures. We hope this book will help ensure that their deeds, and their importance in shaping the history of the Gulf South, are not forgotten.

Contents

Preface to the Fourth Edition   7

Preface   9

Acknowledgements   13

Introduction   15

Timeline   19

Origins of Conflict   23

From Burnt Corn to the Holy Ground   31

Across the Chattahoochee   59

The Path to Horseshoe Bend   73

Securing the Gulf South   97

Conclusion   125

Biographies   129

Original Documents   163

Bibliographic Essay and Notes on Sources   183

Preface to the Fourth Edition

We are pleased and honored to see that *Battle for the Southern Frontier* has merited multiple printings by The History Press. As historians deeply interested in communicating the importance of the Creek War and the War of 1812, we are proud to have played a small role in encouraging greater public awareness of the places and events we attempt to chronicle in the pages of this book. It is truly encouraging to know that there are so many who share our passion for this subject. Since the book's initial publication in the summer of 2008, we have had the privilege of speaking to numerous groups about the topic at a variety of conferences, educational programs and classrooms. The response to our presentations has been overwhelmingly positive. We entered into this project with the goal of filling a void in scholarship available to the general public on this crucial and compelling turning point in American history, and we are humbled to hear the kind words from so many who have let us know that, on some level, we achieved that goal.

There have been updates to several of the historic sites chronicled in the book since the original publishing. Chalmette Battlefield at the Jean Lafitte National Historic Park and Reserve, damaged and temporarily closed due to Hurricane Katrina, has reopened. The park now features a new state-of-the art visitor center, which is a fitting tribute to one of our nation's most glorious military victories. There is important work going on aimed at identifying, interpreting and protecting a variety of other historic sites mentioned in the book, including the sites of Fort Mims, Fort Daniel, Fort Perry, Fort Lawrence, Fort Pitchlynn, Fort Bainbridge and the Battle of the Holy Ground. Others, such as Camp Beaty in northern Alabama, have recently been commemorated with historical markers. We have been informed of interest in a number of other lesser-known sites across the region, as well, and are hopeful that their role in American history can eventually be commemorated in some fashion. We commend the efforts of the many dedicated individuals and organizations that strive to preserve these sites and bring them to life for the education of the public.

We are heartened to see that interest in the bicentennial of the conflicts we chronicle here is growing, and we hope it will be marked by a robust commemoration that spurs new appreciation of their significance by a wide audience. We believe more than ever that there is an urgent need to encourage understanding of our shared heritage in order to create a more informed citizenry, as our society is increasingly consumed with the present and utterly unaware of the history that shaped the development of this nation. We believe strongly in the transformative power of experiencing our hallowed historic sites and assert that few things stir the soul more than connecting with the past through walking the ground where monumental events took place. Unfortunately, these sites are often imperiled and unappreciated. As citizens, we must remember that we have a shared responsibility to save our historic sites for generations to come.

We hope this second edition of *Battle for the Southern Frontier* will continue to assist people in understanding the Creek War and the War of 1812 and exploring the sites on which they took place, and we thank all of the readers who have made its publication possible.

Mike Bunn and Clay Williams
April 2012

Preface

Many conflicts in this nation's history compete for the title of most unknown war, but the Creek War of 1813–14 and the related Southern campaigns of the larger War of 1812 have perhaps the best claim on that notoriety. Little understood because of their brevity, relatively small military forces engaged and complexity, these conflicts dramatically altered the history of the United States. The Creek War and the War of 1812 initiated several far-reaching changes in the Old Southwest, the frontier region that included portions of Georgia, Tennessee, Louisiana, Florida and the future states of Mississippi and Alabama. These wars led to the further development of slave-based cotton agriculture in the region, the forced removal of Native Americans, the securing of large portions of the Gulf South against European powers and, perhaps most importantly, launched the career of one of America's most influential military and political leaders.

Despite the importance of the Creek War and the War of 1812, they have received relatively scant scholarly or public attention, especially when compared to that lavished on the Civil War. The study of that conflict dominates the historiography of the nineteenth-century South. While books examining any number of aspects or events of the Civil War continue to be published yearly, there are precious few studies that examine this earlier, equally formative chapter of Southern history. Perhaps the most striking imbalance in interpretation and understanding of the conflicts is the lack of public markers and memorials at historic sites commemorating the wars' important events. Thankfully, numerous organizations have fought highly publicized battles to save small parcels of land where Civil War battles occurred. Unfortunately, many sites associated with the Creek War and the War of 1812 remain unmarked and underappreciated. In fact, many have already been obliterated by modern development.

For those interested in the study of the past and the preservation of significant historic sites, the news is not all bad. Fortunately, many of the

Fort Madison historic marker. *Photo courtesy of authors.*

Horseshoe Bend National Military Park visitor's center. *Photo courtesy of authors.*

sites related to the Creek War and the larger War of 1812 are located in areas that remain undeveloped today. Historians and preservationists are presented with an enviable opportunity to protect land on which these important events occurred and to educate people about their consequences.

We hope to help address this problem through the publication of this sourcebook. The first of its type, it is meant to serve as an introduction to the study and understanding of the Creek War and the larger War of 1812 and the sites on which they occurred. The book offers a concise overview of the wars, including their causes, major campaigns and battles, influential personalities and their eventual consequences. In addition, it contains an extensive bibliographical essay, as well as the text of several primary documents that are essential to understanding this topic. More importantly, the book documents dozens of sites related to the wars where Native Americans and white settlers lived, forts stood and battles raged.

This publication is a summary of existing scholarship rather than an attempt to break new ground, and we have consequently relied overwhelmingly on secondary sources in its writing. Several capable

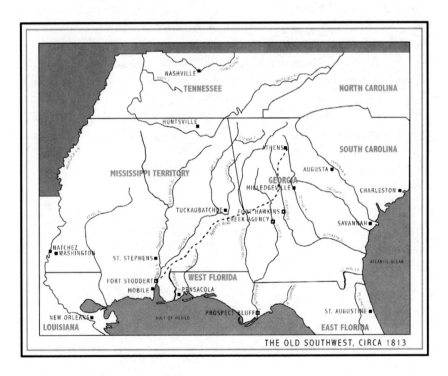

Map by Jessica McCarty.

scholars have already sifted through the original materials to construct an accepted framework for understanding the wars. We hope to build on that framework by creating this sourcebook for the use of the general public. Its strength will be its comprehensiveness because it includes information on a wider variety of aspects of the wars and how they have been commemorated than any previous publication.

As another way to disseminate some of the information in the book and promote the establishment and maintenance of historic markers commemorating the wars, we have launched a website, www. creekwarandwarof1812.com. The site will include photographs of historic sites and markers, descriptions of their significance, maps, a timeline of events and links to other websites that contain additional information. We hope the site will become a resource for those interested in understanding the wars, as well as an information center where updates on the progress toward the placement of markers can be found.

Marking these sites presents an excellent opportunity to not only raise awareness of a crucial, formative era in regional and national history, but it also could serve as a means through which to increase heritage tourism across the South. Discovery of this era in the Gulf South's past is a largely untapped resource, and plans for how to bring attention to these sites for the education of both residents of the region and its visitors are long overdue. Above all, these markers will serve as a small part of the ongoing efforts by a variety of organizations and individuals to preserve a portion of the land on which the Gulf South's past unfolded before it is lost to development. With the attention the conflicts will receive as their 200th anniversary approaches, the time for action is now. If there is one thing that can be learned by observing the struggles to preserve portions of the battlefields on which the Civil War was fought, it is that time is not in our favor. The clock is ticking.

Acknowledgements

The authors are indebted to numerous individuals for their kind assistance during the writing of this book. We owe them, and the many others whom we have no doubt forgotten to mention here, our gratitude.

Those who have provided special assistance and guidance during this project include: Mellda Alexander, the Columbus Museum; Mike Bailey, Fort Morgan State Historic Site; Amia Baker, Ralph B. Draughon Library at Auburn University; Chris Beverly, Clarke County Historical Society; Blanton Blankenship, Fort Morgan State Historic Site; Wanda Braun, St. Stephens Historical Park; Cassie Busby, the Columbus Museum; Glenn Drummond, Macon County Archives; John Gardner; Charlotte Hood; Ove Jensen, Horseshoe Bend National Military Park; Tom Kanon, Tennessee State Library and Archives; Jim Long, St. Stephens Historical Park; John Lyles, the Columbus Library; Jessica McCarty; Teresa Paglione, Natural Resources Conservation Service; Jim Parker, Fort Toulouse-Jackson Park; Greg Pate, E.V. Smith Research Center; Laura Powell; Dalton Royer, the Columbus Library; Dr. Gene Smith, Texas Christian University; Larry Smith; Paul Taylor; James Walker; and Dr. Gregory Waselkov, University of South Alabama.

We also wish to thank the staffs of the Alabama Department of Archives and History, the Auburn University Special Collections and Archives, the Georgia Department of Archives and History, the Historic New Orleans Collection, the Library of Congress, the Mississippi Department of Archives and History, the North Carolina Department of Archives and History, the National Park Service, the Ocmulgee National Monument and the State Archives of Florida.

Finally, we offer a special thanks to our wives, Tonya Bunn and Kym Williams, for their patience and understanding throughout this process.

Introduction

Though interrelated and at times occurring simultaneously, the campaigns of the Creek War and the War of 1812 in the Gulf South are most easily understood when discussed separately. Military operations during the wars took place over a period of almost two years. These actions were all associated with four distinct military campaigns, each involving separate fighting units and occurring in different geographical regions.

Three of these campaigns are almost exclusively associated with the Creek War. Once hostilities between the United States and the Red Sticks began, several loosely coordinated offenses into Creek territory were launched using militia from the Mississippi Territory, Georgia and Tennessee and a small number of regular military forces. These armies, aided by allied Creeks, Cherokees and Choctaws, entered Creek territory from several points. Through the establishment of a series of forts as bases of supply, these armies steadily advanced toward each other, attempting to destroy Creek resistance as they moved. The final campaign of the war, which took place along the Gulf Coast, involved the only actual combat between U.S. and British troops occurring in the region.

The war's first phase included the conflict's beginnings and the campaigns of the Mississippi Territorial militia in present-day southwestern Alabama. After the war's initial battle in July 1813, area settlers fled to several hastily built stockades in anticipation of further hostilities. The infamous attack on one of these stockades, Fort Mims, brought the war into the nation's consciousness. This first phase of the war culminated in the destruction of the village known as the Holy Ground, an important base of operations for the Red Sticks supposedly impervious to assault by whites.

The second campaign occurred primarily in east-central Alabama as part of the raids into Creek territory by troops under the command of Generals John Floyd and David Adams. These troops, mostly Georgia

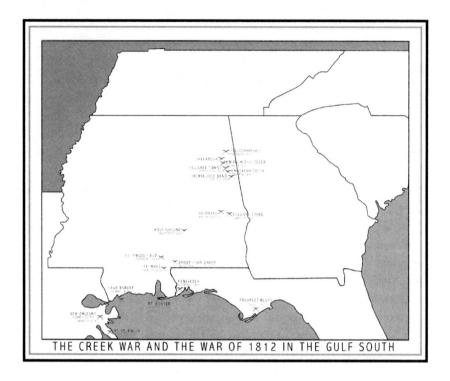

THE CREEK WAR AND THE WAR OF 1812 IN THE GULF SOUTH

Map by Jessica McCarty.

militia assisted by a small number of allied Creeks, departed central Georgia for Creek villages near the Chattahoochee and Tallapoosa Rivers. During late 1813 and early 1814, these armies fought two large-scale battles at Autossee and Calabee Creek and a number of smaller skirmishes. These battles weakened Red Stick strength in the region and resulted in the destruction of Autossee, one of the largest Creek towns.

The last campaign of the Creek War involved fighting between Red Stick Creeks and troops under the overall command of General Andrew Jackson. Primarily men from Tennessee who responded to the call for volunteers after Fort Mims, these troops and allied Cherokees and Creeks initially fought as part of two armies; one personally led by Jackson and another led by General John Cocke. Overcoming a series of setbacks and the near mutiny of his troops on more than one occasion, Jackson's force fought a series of battles in the fall of 1813 and the spring of 1814, including Tallushatchee, Talladega and Emuckfau. This campaign culminated in the destruction of the Red Sticks as a military force at Horseshoe Bend. In the aftermath, Jackson forced the Creeks to sign the landmark Treaty of Fort Jackson.

The final campaign involved conflicts between U.S., Spanish and British troops in the Gulf South. After securing the surrender of the Creeks, Jackson turned his attention to halting the impending British invasion. He moved quickly to prevent the British from using Spanish bases on the Gulf Coast for offensive operations, simultaneously eliminating the possibility of a British alliance with the Creeks. In these operations, American forces repulsed a British attack against Mobile and captured Pensacola in the fall of 1814. Finally, Jackson repulsed the British advance on New Orleans, winning one of the most celebrated military victories in American history.

Timeline

September–October 1811   Tecumseh travels among the Creeks and delivers an address at Tuckaubatchee, the site of the annual Creek council meeting.

Spring 1812   Several white settlers are killed by Red Stick Creeks in Mississippi Territory and Tennessee.

April 1812   The United States claims Mobile and portions of West Florida.

June 1812   The United States declares war on Great Britain.

January–April 1813   Andrew Jackson leads an expedition to Natchez for the defense of the New Orleans region. After being ordered by General Wilkinson to disband his army, Jackson leads his troops back to Tennessee along the Natchez Trace, acquiring the nickname "Old Hickory" in the process.

April 1813   Red Stick Creeks are executed for the murder of white settlers near the mouth of the Ohio River earlier in the year. U.S. troops, under General James Wilkinson, seize Mobile from the Spanish.

May 1813	Red Stick Creeks make the first of three visits to Spanish-held Pensacola to obtain war supplies.
Summer 1813	Several forts are constructed in the Tensaw Region for the defense of the settlers.
July 27, 1813	Battle of Burnt Corn Creek.
August 30, 1813	Battle of Fort Mims.
September 1, 1813	Kimbell-James Massacre.
September 2, 1813	Battle of Fort Sinquefield.
September 1813	Authorities in Tennessee, Georgia and Mississippi Territory call out militia to restore order on the frontier.
November 3, 1813	Battle of Tallushatchee.
November 9, 1813	Battle of Talladega.
November 1813–January 1814	Andrew Jackson struggles with supply and enlistment problems.
November 12, 1813	The Canoe Fight.
November 18, 1813	Hillabee Massacre.
November 29, 1813	Battle of Autossee.
December 23, 1813	Battle of Holy Ground.
January 22, 1814	Battle of Emuckfau Creek.
January 24, 1814	Battle of Enitachopco Creek.

January 27, 1814	Battle of Calabee Creek.
March 27, 1814	Battle of Horseshoe Bend.
April 1814	Fort Jackson is established.
May 1814	The British arrive in Florida and begin recruitment of Red Stick Creeks.
August 9, 1814	The signing of the Treaty of Fort Jackson.
August 1814	Andrew Jackson moves his headquarters to Mobile to prepare for a British attack.
September 12–15, 1814	First Battle of Fort Bowyer.
November 7, 1814	Andrew Jackson seizes Pensacola from the Spanish.
December 1, 1814	Andrew Jackson arrives in New Orleans.
December 14, 1814	Battle of Lake Borgne.
December 17–23, 1814	The British army is transported from the Gulf of Mexico to the vicinity of New Orleans.
December 23, 1814	Andrew Jackson attacks the British encampment.
December 24, 1814	The Treaty of Ghent is signed.
December 28, 1814	British "reconnaissance in force" of American lines outside of New Orleans.
January 1, 1815	The British artillery bombards American lines outside New Orleans.

January 8, 1815	Battle of New Orleans.
January 9–18, 1815	The British bombard Fort St. Philip.
February 11, 1815	Second Battle of Fort Bowyer.
June 1815	The British abandon Prospect Bluff.
July 1816	"Negro Fort" at Prospect Bluff is destroyed.

Origins of Conflict

For decades prior to the Creek War, Americans, Creek Indians and the Spanish had maintained an uneasy truce as they each claimed portions of the Gulf South. Pressure on this shaky arrangement steadily mounted during the early nineteenth century as the region witnessed increased American migration, strained efforts at cultural adaptation on the part of the Creeks and international intrigue associated with the Spanish and their newfound allies, the British. When violence finally erupted, it quickly spiraled into a cataclysmic war that would alter the course of American history.

Creek lands were in the center of the hotly contested Old Southwest in the early 1800s. The Creek Nation occupied territory located primarily in what are today the states of Alabama and Georgia, with the great majority of the Creeks' ancestral lands lying within the limits of the newly formed Mississippi Territory. To their west and north lay the lands of the Choctaws, Chickasaws and Cherokees; farther north lay the state of Tennessee. To the east, Creek lands were bordered by the state of Georgia, and to the south lay Spanish-controlled West Florida. As a consequence of their location, the Creeks had long been courted by both the Americans and the Spanish. While Americans jealously looked upon rich Creek lands as perfectly suited for large-scale agriculture, the Spanish simply hoped to use the Creek Nation as a buffer to American encroachment into their territory.

As each party pursued its own interests, conflict inevitably resulted. Spanish efforts to win the loyalty of the Creeks angered Americans, many of whom suspected the Spanish of deliberately inciting the natives to violence on unprotected American frontier settlements. Further, many viewed the continued illegal British trade with the Creeks—much of which was carried on in Spanish territory with colonial officials seemingly unable or unwilling to halt it—as a glaring threat to American safety. Just as importantly, Americans were alarmed that Mobile Bay and the

Map by Jessica McCarty.

Alabama-Tombigbee River system, one of the easiest routes of invasion into the Southern United States, lay in foreign hands.

Concerns grew over British attempts to undermine the safety of the American Gulf South frontier with the outbreak of the War of 1812. Though many of the provocations listed by President James Madison in his call for war—including the longstanding British policy of impressing U.S. sailors and Britain's refusal to evacuate forts on American soil per the terms of the treaty ending the Revolutionary War—were only peripheral concerns of most Americans living in the Gulf South, the threat of a British-Spanish alliance that would enlist the support of Southern tribes was one of their greatest fears. The British were known to have instigated natives to violence against American settlers in the Northwest, and their increasingly close relationship with the Spanish on the Southern frontier caused considerable alarm.

Concerned over Spanish and British complicity in growing Creek hostility, the United States eventually ordered General James Wilkinson to seize Spanish Florida west of the Perdido River in the spring of 1813. Americans had argued for years that this territory was rightfully part of the United States by virtue of the terms of the Louisiana Purchase. Realizing the futility of resistance, the overmatched Spanish garrison at Fort Charlotte (Fuerta Carlota) in Mobile surrendered without a fight on April 13, 1813. The seizure was the first serious altercation between U.S. and Spanish forces in the region during the War of 1812, but it would not be the last. Before the War of 1812 was over, there would be not only additional seizures of Spanish land in the region, but also a showdown between American and British forces that would settle the matter of European intervention in the affairs of the Gulf Coast once and for all.

Caught in the middle of this international intrigue were the Creeks, who had been the special focus of a concerted American effort at assimilation since the 1790s. From his agency on the Flint River, federal agent Benjamin Hawkins spearheaded the American government's effort to convince the Creeks to adopt tenets of white society in place of traditional ways that were viewed as incompatible with modern reality. Essential to this plan was the undertaking of staple agriculture in place of hunting; the rationale being that the Creeks would need less land to live on and vast expanses of their former hunting grounds could therefore be opened to American settlement. The plan, based on cold calculation as much as any altruistic motives, ultimately served to highlight growing divisions in Creek society. The Creeks who embraced the plan were forced to simultaneously and completely reject their ancestral way of life. Furthermore, adoption of the plan by only portions of the Creek population caused previously nonexistent divisions in tribal society, based on ownership of property for agricultural purposes, to develop.

Further straining Creek-American relations was the construction of the Federal Road. A government-sponsored route through the heart of Creek territory, the road connected central Georgia with American settlements in the Tensaw region between the lower Tombigbee and Alabama Rivers. Many Creeks watched with growing apprehension as thousands of white settlers made their way through the Creeks' homeland over the route.

Members of the Creek Nation were divided over what course of action to take regarding American interference in their way of life and encroachment on their lands. The Creek Nation was a loose confederacy of tribes, roughly grouped into two geographically oriented factions. For decades, Creeks had intermingled and intermarried with Americans and Europeans to the point that many leading chiefs could claim as much European as Native American ancestry. Many Upper Creeks, living in what is today north-central and northeast Alabama, gradually began to perceive this situation as acquiescence in a wholesale destruction of their culture. Relatively more removed from regular interaction with Americans and far less assimilated with their culture, these Creeks felt increasingly isolated in their struggle to retain their cultural and territorial identities. Many Lower Creeks, on the other hand, occupying lands stretching from modern-day central Georgia to southwest Alabama, generally believed it in their best interest to befriend Americans and negotiate with them to maintain their territorial integrity.

Into this tense situation in 1811 entered Tecumseh, the proverbial spark that would ultimately ignite the smoldering tinderbox that was the Old Southwest. A Shawnee who claimed to have familial ties to the Creeks, Tecumseh was a native of the Great Lakes Region and the leading figure in Native American resistance to American settlement in the Old Northwest. He believed an Indian confederacy was the only way to ensure the survival of native tribes in the face of mounting encroachment on their lands by Americans, and he set out with his brother, Tenskwatawa (The Prophet), to share his plan. Assisted by prophets who helped transform his political vision into a religious crusade, he called for a halt to American encroachment and a return to traditional ways of life. In the summer and fall of 1811, he traveled throughout the Southeast in an attempt to rally the Chickasaws, Choctaws and Creeks to his cause. He was largely unsuccessful, except with all but a portion of the Upper Creeks, many of whom he addressed at their annual council meeting at Tuckaubatchee in modern-day central Alabama. Those encouraged by what he said became even more supportive when his prophecies regarding the appearance of a comet and the occurrence of an earthquake seemed to be fulfilled shortly after his visit. Creeks who supported Tecumseh came to be known as Red Sticks in reference to the traditional color of Creek wooden war clubs, and they became determined to halt further American settlement in their territory and the adoption of American ways of life among their tribe. Conflict between Red Sticks and Creeks friendly to American interests soon erupted into a civil war that further fractured Creek society.

Violence between Red Sticks and American settlers first flared up in the spring of 1812. During that year, Red Sticks launched several attacks on American settlers. News of one such attack on a settlement along the Duck River in Tennessee, resulting in the killing of seven people and the capture of Martha Crawley, caused widespread indignation. Agent Hawkins took swift action to bring all the killers to justice and eliminate the rebellion before it gained momentum. Several participants in these

Tecumseh entering the Creek Council. *From George Cary Eggleston,* Red Eagle and the Wars With the Creek Indians of Alabama.

attacks, including the leader, Little Warrior, were executed by Creeks who agreed to carry out Hawkins's orders to ensure that justice was done.

Despite these actions, the violence continued to escalate in 1813. In February, several American families were brutally murdered near the mouth of the Ohio River. One of the victims, a pregnant woman, had her unborn child cut from her and placed on a stake. In accordance with Hawkins's orders that the killers be apprehended, Chief William McIntosh and others found and killed the culprits. In reprisal, Red Sticks later murdered several members of McIntosh's party. Outraged at their fellow Creeks for carrying out Hawkins's orders and steadily growing bolder and more determined in their plans, Red Sticks began to kill chiefs who were viewed as friendly to the United States. They also began regular communication with the Spanish in Pensacola in an attempt to obtain arms. In July 1813, they laid siege to the town of Tuckaubatchee, the residence of prominent Creek leader Big Warrior. With open warfare seemingly inevitable, American officials began to mobilize forces to respond in case of emergency.

American settlers in frontier communities bordering Creek territory were in a panic by the summer of 1813. Nowhere was this state of alarm more pronounced than in the Tensaw District. Located in the southwestern portion of Creek territory, the Tensaw region was a virtual island of American settlement with a large population of mixed-blood

Creeks who were increasingly viewed with contempt by the Red Sticks. The nearest sizable town, Mobile, lay well to the south. More importantly, it was separated by several hundred miles of wilderness from the seat of the Mississippi territorial government in Washington, near Natchez, along the Mississippi River. Keenly aware of their precarious situation, Tensaw settlers began to construct a series of stockades for their protection as they prepared for the inevitable conflict.

Historic Sites

The Creek Agency

Located on the banks of the Flint River, the Creek Agency was the headquarters of Agent Benjamin Hawkins. Hawkins lived there with his family, slaves and small staff during the war. He died there in 1816.

A marker for the agency stands about a quarter mile north of the Flint River on Georgia Highway 128, near the town of Roberta in Crawford County, Georgia.

The Creek Agency historical marker. *Photo courtesy of authors.*

The Federal Road

The Federal Road ran through Creek territory and connected central Georgia with the Mobile area. The federal government obtained permission to construct the road—originally intended as a postal route to facilitate faster communication with the city of New Orleans—in the 1805 Treaty of Washington. Construction began in 1806. Recognizing the military importance of the route once tensions with Great Britain escalated, the federal government ordered the widening of the road in 1811. It eventually connected Fort Stoddert, on the Mobile River in current-day Alabama, and Fort Wilkinson, near the Oconee River in Georgia. The road became a primary route for settlers entering the Mississippi Territory and one of the main points of contention between the Creek Nation and the United States.

The route, which roughly follows U.S. Highway 80 from Macon, Georgia, to Montgomery, Alabama, and Interstate 65 from Montgomery to just north of Mobile, Alabama, is denoted by several historic markers.

Fort Carlota (Fort Charlotte)

Fort Carlota was the seat of Spanish government in Mobile. The fort, located on the site of the French Fort Condé, had been a British outpost

A section of the original Federal Road in Macon County, Alabama. *Photo courtesy of authors.*

prior to Spain's seizure of the area during the American Revolution. In an effort to secure possession of the disputed region of West Florida, General James Wilkinson seized the fort without a fight in April 1813.

A reconstruction of Fort Condé today sits on the site of Fort Charlotte in downtown Mobile, Alabama. The fort features a museum focusing on the history of the site, and it serves as a welcome center for the city of Mobile.

Mobile

Mobile, founded in 1702 to serve as the capital of the French colony of Louisiana, was one of the largest population and trading centers in the Gulf Coast region during the Creek War and the War of 1812. Defended by Fort Carlota, the city was the center of Spanish colonial authority in the region until it was seized by General James Wilkinson in the spring of 1813. Many settlers of the Tensaw District fled to Mobile for safety at the onset of the Creek War. The city became the target of the British during their Gulf Coast offensive of the War of 1812, and they twice attempted to capture it. While the first ended in failure, the second was halted by news of the treaty ending the war.

Today, a reproduction of Fort Condé, the first fort built on the site of Fort Carlota, stands in downtown Mobile as a monument to the city's colonial past. A block away is the Museum of Mobile, which contains exhibits focusing on the city's role in the Creek War and the War of 1812.

Tuckaubatchee (Tookabachi or Tuckabachi)

Tuckaubatchee was a major Creek population and political center located along the west bank of the Tallapoosa River in current-day Elmore County, Alabama, near its confluence with the Coosa River. The town was the site of the Creek annual council, where Tecumseh made his impassioned speech in the fall of 1811 urging the Creeks to take up arms against white men. A "peace" town for the Creeks, Red Sticks besieged and burned it during the Creek civil war.

The town site is located south of the town of Tallassee, Alabama, off Highway 229. It is unmarked and lies on private land. A marker commemorating the town stands near the city hall in the town of Tallassee.

From Burnt Corn to the Holy Ground

"Our hearts were torn with contending passions, by turns with grief and burning with revenge."
—*Captain J.P. Kennedy to Brigadier General Ferdinand L. Claiborne following the Battle of Fort Mims, September 9, 1813*

Long-simmering tensions erupted into open conflict between American and Red Stick forces in July 1813. On the tenth of that month, a large group of Red Stick warriors headed by Peter McQueen, Josiah Francis and High Head Jim left their encampment at the Holy Ground and headed for Pensacola, where they hoped to obtain arms and ammunition from the Spanish. Their mission soon became general knowledge among the settlements of the Tensaw region—the relatively heavily settled area just north of Mobile along the Alabama and Tombigbee Rivers and their distributaries—after they burned the plantation homes of prominent Creeks Sam Moniac and James Cornells along the way. Residents of Pensacola friendly to American interests probably also reported the activity of the Red Sticks upon their arrival in the town. A state of alarm prevailed once settlers realized they intended to use any supplies they received to attack Americans instead of other Creeks. Without awaiting instructions from Mississippi territorial militia commander Ferdinand L. Claiborne, Colonel James Caller, the ranking officer in the local militia, hastily called out his command and set out in search of the group.

Unbeknownst to Caller, the Red Sticks' excursion was not nearly as successful as they would have liked. McQueen's party, the second Red Stick group to seek the aid of the Spanish that summer, had gone to Pensacola in large part in response to the perceived invitation of Spanish leadership, whom they believed stood ready to support a campaign against the Americans. While the Spanish indeed viewed support of the Red Sticks as a way to assist their own defense of Pensacola against

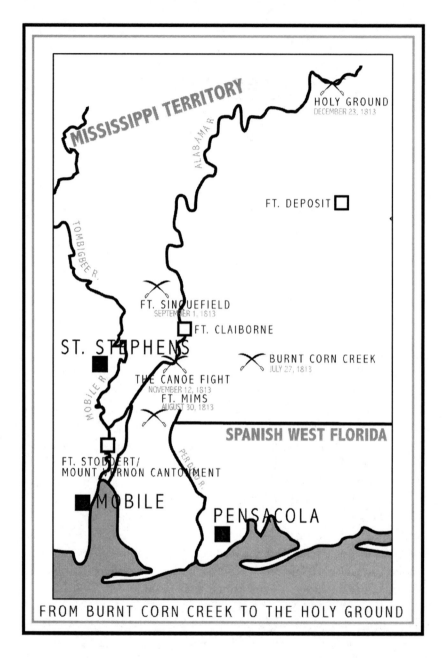

Map by Jessica McCarty.

any possible offensive by the Americans, they were not prepared to aid such an effort materially at the moment. Despite resorting to threatening the Spanish if they did not comply with their requests, the Red Sticks ultimately left Pensacola with only some gunpowder, lead, food and blankets. Some believe they may have also obtained a small number of weapons from area merchants. Very few of the Red Sticks returning from Pensacola, however, are believed to have had firearms.

Caller's force of about 180 troops spotted McQueen's encampment on the morning of July 27, 1813, near Burnt Corn Creek, close to the modern boundary line between Conecuh and Escambia Counties in Alabama. Around 11:00 a.m., Caller ordered a surprise attack. Descending a small hill toward the Red Sticks, the American militia scattered them in disorder across the creek. While they stopped to inspect the packhorses they had just captured, however, some of the Red Sticks regrouped in a nearby swamp and launched a counterattack. The American militia fled in terror. A small number of men, under the command of Sam Dale, Dixon Bailey and Benjamin Smoot, rallied and held out long enough to prevent the affair from becoming a complete rout. Disorganized, Caller's militia straggled back home and disbanded. The troops were in such disarray on their retreat that even Caller himself became lost and was not found until over two weeks later.

Despite the relatively small number of casualties—two killed and fifteen wounded of the American militia and about the same for the Red Sticks—the battle was a disaster for the Americans. As their victory seemed to confirm some of Tecumseh's prophecies, the Red Sticks gained a newfound confidence in their martial abilities. Simultaneously, American forces had been embarrassed and humbled. As the ensuing panic among American settlements of the Tensaw region became general, many terrified residents fled to the safety of their makeshift forts and awaited the inevitable Red Stick offensive.

Along with established forts at St. Stephens and Fort Stoddert, these fortified positions formed the Tensaw region's primary line of defense. Over fifteen of them were in various stages of construction in the region at the time of the Battle of Burnt Corn Creek. Essentially hastily built palisade walls or fortified homesteads, these forts were constructed to accommodate settlers from their immediate vicinity in case of attack. They were spaced at convenient intervals between frontier communities, and their names—such as Mims, Sinquefield, Madison, Glass and Landrum—came from the property owners on whose land they were constructed. Upon arriving at Fort Stoddert, General Ferdinand

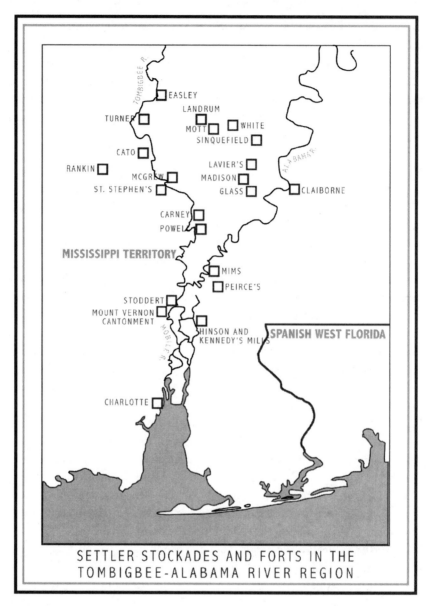

Map by Jessica McCarty.

Claiborne quickly deduced that it was impractical to defend all of these positions at the same time. Instead, he chose to divide his forces among five strategic stockades and prepared to shift troops to where they were needed in the event an attack occurred.

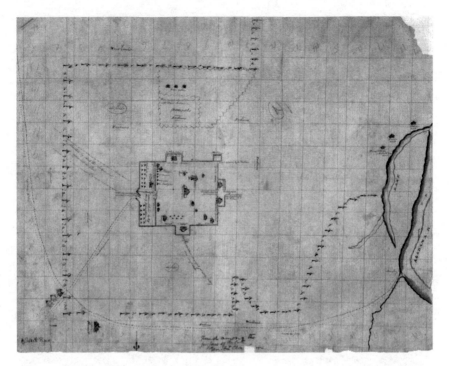

A map of Fort Mims and environs, by Ferdinand L. Claiborne. *Courtesy of the Alabama Department of Archives and History.*

One of the largest of these stockades, and the location of one of the largest detachment of Claiborne's troops, was Fort Mims. The fortification had been built around several structures on the plantation of prominent Tensaw District planter Samuel Mims and enclosed about one acre of land. Fort Mims featured split log walls, two gates and a partially constructed blockhouse, in addition to the Mims' plantation structures and several rude cabins constructed by area settlers who had come there for safety. By the end of August 1813, the fort held approximately 250 settlers, just over 100 troops of the Mississippi Territorial militia and about 40 local militiamen under the overall command of Major Daniel Beasley.

The Red Sticks chose Fort Mims as one of their first objectives in their offensive. Seeking revenge for the surprise attack at Burnt Corn, they targeted the fort in large part because of the many Creeks living there who had either assisted Caller's troops or simply refused to join their cause. As many as one thousand Red Sticks gathered near Flat Creek in present-day Monroe County, Alabama, in late August to plan for the assault. They determined on a two-prong strategy of attack. A group of

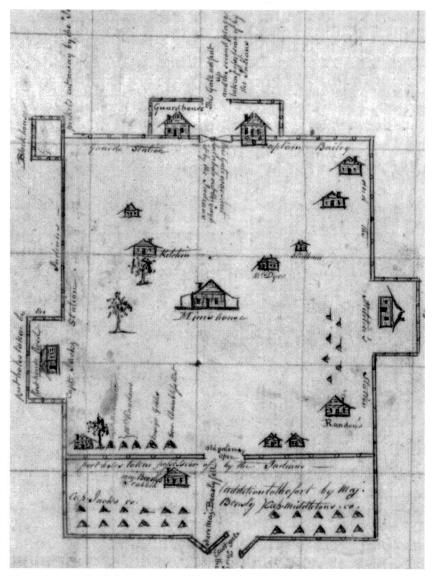

Detail from Claiborne's map of Fort Mims. *Courtesy of the Alabama Department of Archives and History.*

approximately seven hundred warriors, under the command of William Weatherford (Red Eagle), Paddy Walsh, Peter McQueen and others, was to stealthily begin an advance toward Fort Mims, about fifty miles distant, while a smaller group, led by Josiah Francis, was to move on nearby Fort Sinquefield. Though several individuals detected their movement and reported it to Major Beasley, he refused to believe that an attack on his post was being planned. Even in his last letter to General Claiborne, written only a few hours before the Red Stick attack, he expressed no awareness of his dangerous predicament. As a consequence of his false sense of confidence, the fort lay totally unprepared for the Red Sticks.

The Battle of Fort Mims began at noon on August 30, 1813. Hundreds of Red Stick warriors, concealed only four hundred yards from the fort, rose and ran silently toward it at the command of one of their leaders. They went unnoticed until they were within a few steps of the stockade, and they took those inside by complete surprise. Major Beasley became one of the first casualties of the battle, being struck down as he desperately tried to close the fort's open eastern gate. Following a plan formulated by William Weatherford, the Red Sticks quickly took control of most of the loopholes in the fort's walls to prevent return fire. The occupants of Fort Mims were nearly overwhelmed and were forced to flee to the interior structures of the fort to organize a defense. They finally managed to stem the initial Red Stick onslaught after about two hours of vicious fighting. After briefly retreating to regroup, the Red Sticks launched a second assault. Weatherford allegedly protested this second attack to no avail.

In the massacre that followed, Fort Mims was destroyed and the great majority of those inside were killed. Almost immediately, the Red Sticks began to set fire to the structures inside the fort, and the garrison was

"The Attack on Fort Mims." *Courtesy of the Museum of Mobile.*

gradually corralled into one bastion. Red Sticks brutally murdered and scalped hundreds of men, women and children as the fighting wore on. Only a handful of those in the fort, no more than 30, managed to make a desperate escape. The fighting ceased around five o'clock in the afternoon. Because of their heavy losses, the Red Sticks decided to abandon any further offensive in the area. Estimates of their casualties vary widely, ranging from as few as 100 to over 300. Nearly 250 of those in Fort Mims were killed, and about 100—mostly women, children and slaves—were taken prisoner. Territorial District Judge Harry Toulmin, the most prominent federal official in the region, notified General Flournoy of what had occurred the next day and began interviewing survivors as they straggled into Fort Stoddert.

The other Red Stick war party that had met at Flat Creek, headed by Josiah Francis, struck only days after the affair at Fort Mims. On September 1, Francis's warriors murdered a dozen members of the Kimbell and James families at a home near Bassett's Creek, about a mile from Fort Sinquefield. Incredibly, two of the few survivors of the attack included a woman who had been scalped and her infant son. Colonel Joseph Carson, at nearby Fort Madison, sent a force of eleven men under Lieutenant James Bailey to bury the dead the next day.

The bodies had just been interred near Fort Sinquefield around noon when the Red Stick war party, at first mistaken by one of Sinquefield's inhabitants for a flock of wild turkeys, rushed the fort. Several women doing laundry outside the fort's walls at the time of the charge made a narrow escape when Isaac Hayden, a resident of the fort, famously turned some hunting dogs on the attackers. His tactic saved the lives of all but one of the women and allowed just enough time for the gates of the stockade to be closed. Though garrisoned by only fifteen men and their families, the inhabitants of Fort Sinquefield held off the attackers for over two hours with the loss of only one man. Eleven Red Sticks are believed to have been killed and an unknown number injured in the encounter.

Those in Fort Sinquefield made their way to Fort Madison soon after the battle, where they found residents from Forts Glass and Lavier had also fled. Nineteen-year-old Jeremiah Austill carried news of the attack to General Claiborne at Mount Vernon and then returned with an order from the general that the fort be abandoned and its inhabitants make their way to St. Stephens. Several hundred people left immediately, but a large number remained and made improvements to the fort. Notable among these was a forty-foot-high pine torch, which helped prevent a nighttime surprise attack by Red Sticks. Though several smaller skirmishes between settlers and Red

Hayden charging the Red Sticks with hunting dogs. *From George Cary Eggleston,* Red Eagle and the Wars With the Creek Indians of Alabama.

Sticks would be fought in the area over the coming months, the Red Sticks would never again launch a significant offensive in the Tensaw region.

News of the Red Stick strike stunned the nation. Americans were horrified and indignant at the scale of the atrocity, and many suspected Spanish or British interlopers as the masterminds of the assault. For a few weeks, a bitter controversy over who to blame for the unprecedented disaster raged. To the thousands of troops immediately raised to put down the rebellion, however, the name "Fort Mims" became a rallying cry for revenge. Almost before the last of the victims of the attack had been buried in early September, plans for reprisal were put in motion.

Following a previously designed plan, armies from the Mississippi Territory, Tennessee and Georgia attempted to simultaneously converge on Red Stick territory from different directions. General Thomas Flournoy, in command of the Seventh Military District, which included the Mississippi Territory, moved first. He ordered General Ferdinand L. Claiborne to move north from St. Stephens with several hundred militiamen and eliminate any Red Stick resistance he encountered. Eventually, troops from the United States Infantry reinforced him.

Claiborne's offensive initially failed to bring about any substantial engagement, though, as his command instead became involved in several isolated skirmishes. One of the largest of these occurred in mid-October,

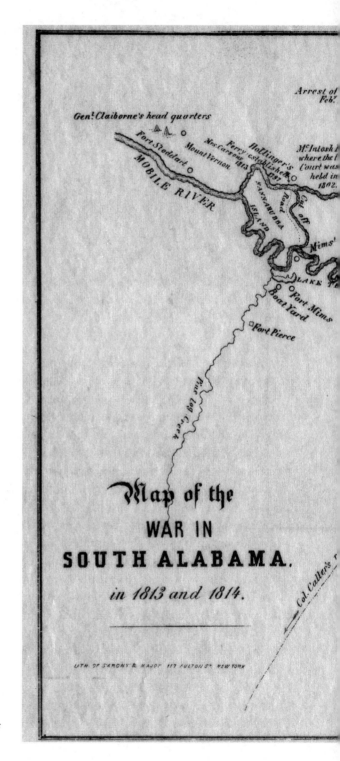

Map of the war in South
Alabama. *Courtesy of the
Alabama Department of Archives
and History.*

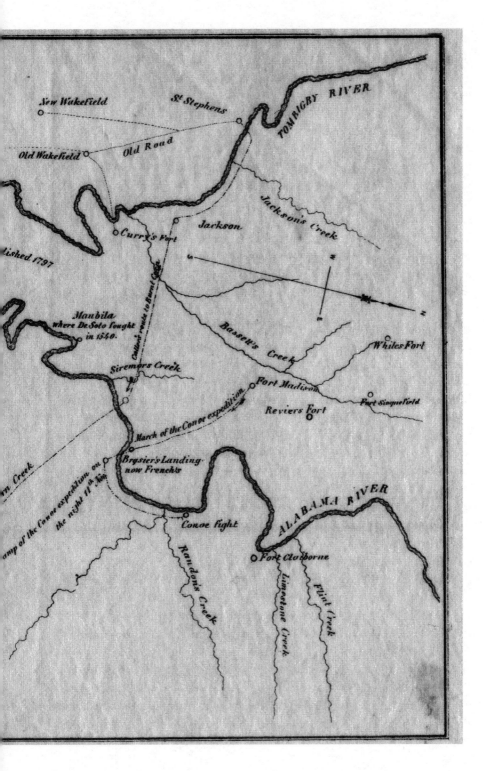

when Red Sticks ambushed a group of about twenty-five militiamen near the abandoned Easley's Fort along Bashi Creek in present-day Clarke County, Alabama. Four Americans and approximately ten Red Sticks perished. Claiborne's efforts at reprisal only resulted in additional, smaller skirmishes. Perhaps the most significant event to impact Claiborne's army during this time was the departure of Major Thomas Hinds's dragoons, whom General Flournoy dismissed for insubordination. On their return to Natchez, and without orders, they massacred a small band of Creeks they encountered at an abandoned plantation.

One of the expeditions of a detachment of American troops in November 1813 has become one of the enduring legends of the Creek War. On the twelfth of that month, a force of about seventy men, sent from Fort Madison to reconnoiter, encountered small groups of Red Sticks along the Alabama River. A running skirmish ensued. During a pause in the action in the late morning, the Americans spotted a large canoe containing eleven warriors descending the river. Despite the odds, and the fact that most of the American force remained on the bank of the river opposite him, Captain Sam Dale determined to meet the group in a small dugout with only three other men: Privates Jeremiah Austill and James Smith, and a black man named Caesar. Two warriors jumped from the large canoe before Dale's boat could get underway, one of whom Private Smith shot. Caesar paddled the Americans' canoe alongside the Red Sticks', and the battle began. Using knives, bayonets, gun butts and paddles, Dale and the two privates killed the entire Indian party in a brief, but desperate fight. While an unknown number of Red Sticks watched the scene from the banks of the river with disillusionment, the American spectators witnessed the creation of a hero in Dale. The encounter proved to be just the sort of morale builder the American troops needed at the moment.

The next day, November 13, 1813, Claiborne moved his army north in preparation for an assault on the Holy Ground. A fortified town of over two hundred buildings, Holy Ground was located on a bluff in a curve of the Alabama River. It served as a home for Red Stick prophet leaders, as well as a base of supply and place of refuge for warriors. According to the prophet Josiah Francis, the town had been rendered invincible to attack by Americans through a magical ring of defense encircling it. Any enemy who approached the town, believed the prophets, would instantly drop dead.

After being reinforced by about fifty friendly Choctaws under Pushmataha, the American army built Fort Claiborne on a bluff overlooking the Alabama River to serve as a base of operations. By the end of the month, Claiborne

The Canoe Fight. *From J.F.H. Claiborne,* Life and Times of General Sam Dale, the Mississippi Partisan. *Courtesy of the Mississippi Department of Archives and History.*

was joined by Lieutenant Colonel Gilbert C. Russell's Third Regiment of U.S. Infantry. On December 13, Claiborne's force of regulars, volunteers, militia and friendly Choctaws, approximately one thousand men in all, departed for the Holy Ground. Claiborne halted about thirty miles from the town to construct a supply depot named Fort Deposit. Leaving the army's wagons, cannon and sick under a small guard, the army resumed its advance on December 22, 1813.

As they approached the town the next day, Claiborne organized his command into three columns to facilitate an encirclement of the town. Colonel Joseph Carson's Mississippi Territory Volunteers were on the right, Captain Benjamin Smoot's battalion of militia and Pushmataha's battalion of Choctaws were on the left and Colonel Gilbert C. Russell's Third Infantry, headed personally by Claiborne, occupied the center. Claiborne ordered Major Cassels's cavalry to advance west along the riverbank to complete the entrapment.

The Red Sticks, under the command of William Weatherford, had detected the approach of the Americans and sent the women and children of the village across the river to safety. The small force left to defend the town, which included several blacks, prepared to make their stand behind a low wall made of stacked wood. Owing to a shortage of arms and ammunition, though, many were forced to fight with only bows and arrows.

The battle began about noon. Only Carson's men on Clairborne's right became substantially engaged in the affair. They made first contact with the town's defenders and ultimately drove them back, forcing a disorderly retreat. As a result of unexpected difficulties encountered in crossing the swamp that lay to the west of the town, Cassels's cavalry had been unable to reach its assigned position, and most of the warriors escaped through this gap in the American lines. One of the last to retreat, Weatherford made a dramatic escape that has become engrained in myth. While under fire, he jumped his trusted horse, Arrow, off a fifteen-foot-high bluff into the river. In a hail of bullets, he disappeared into the forest on the opposite bank of the Alabama. The entire affair lasted about an hour. Suffering only one casualty, Americans killed between twenty and thirty Red Sticks.

After the battle, General Claiborne permitted the town to be plundered by the Choctaw warriors before ordering it to be burned. To the horror and outrage of his troops, they found in the middle of the town a pole on which were hung as many as three hundred scalps, presumably from the victims of Fort Mims. Owing to the Creek practice of cutting scalps into multiple pieces to increase the number of trophies, this number does not necessarily correlate to the number of those killed at Fort Mims.

On the day after the battle, Claiborne's command moved upriver toward the plantations of William Weatherford and his brother-in-law, Sam Moniac, a Creek leader who opposed the Red Sticks and actually helped guide Claiborne's force to the Holy Ground. Along the way, they fought and killed three of the Shawnee prophets who had resided at Holy Ground. Soon afterward, they discovered conclusive proof of Spanish complicity in the Creek uprising in a letter found in Weatherford's house. In the letter, the Spanish governor in Pensacola, Gonzalez Manrique, expressed his congratulations to the Red Sticks for their victory at Fort Mims and counseled against their proposed suggestion of destroying Mobile. Short on supplies, the American army began its move back to Fort Deposit on Christmas Day after burning the Red Stick refugee settlements located near the Weatherford and Moniac plantations. After a short stay, the men continued on to Fort Claiborne, where the militia and volunteers were mustered out of service since their terms of enlistment had expired.

At that moment, Colonel Russell's Third Regiment at Fort Claiborne remained as the only organized American military force of any size in the region. General Thomas Pinckney, now in overall command of the war from his base in Charleston, South Carolina, ordered Russell to stockpile supplies in anticipation of the arrival of General Andrew

Red Eagle's leap. *From George Cary Eggleston,* Red Eagle and the Wars With the Creek Indians of Alabama.

Jackson's Tennessee army and General John Floyd's Georgia troops. In the meantime, Russell sent a group of friendly Choctaws and Chickasaws under John McKee on a raid of Red Stick towns along the Black Warrior River. The expedition got as far as the site of modern-day Tuscaloosa, only to find the villages abandoned.

Back at Fort Claiborne, Russell, reinforced and resupplied, determined to launch his own offensive. He set out with six hundred men on February 1, 1814, in search of Red Stick towns on the Cahaba River. He found the towns after a grueling march, only to discover that they had also been abandoned. To make matters worse, a supply detachment, headed by Captain James E. Dinkins, was nowhere to be found. After sending a search party, headed by Lieutenant James M. Wilcox, to find the detachment, Russell headed back to Fort Claiborne. Despite being forced to eat some of their horses to survive on the journey, the army eventually returned intact. Red Sticks ambushed Wilcox's ill-fated search party, killing its leader.

The fighting between American and Red Stick forces in the Tensaw region was effectively at an end. Having disrupted Red Stick communications with Pensacola and having scattered any remaining pockets of resistance in the area, Russell's troops eventually played an even more critical role in the overall success of the war by providing much-needed supplies to the other American armies sent to put down the Red Stick rebellion. With order restored in the region where the war had begun, the focus of attention turned to the north and east.

Historic Sites

Bashi Skirmish

In October 1813, a small force of militia was ambushed by Red Sticks at Bashi Creek, less than two miles from the abandoned Fort Easley.

A historic marker for the Bashi Skirmish is reputedly located on Woods Bluff Road, a short distance off County Road 69 in northwestern Clarke County, Alabama.

Burnt Corn Creek

The first full-scale battle between American and Red Stick forces was fought on July 27, 1813, at the Battle of Burnt Corn Creek. Burnt Corn Creek is a tributary of the Conecuh River, which flows through Conecuh and Escambia Counties in Alabama. In the encounter, a band of Red Stick warriors returning from Pensacola defeated militia under the command of James Caller.

The site of the Battle of Burnt Corn Creek lies just inside Escambia County near the southern border of Conecuh County, though the exact location of the battlefield is still the subject of some debate. The site is unmarked.

Fort Carney

Fort Carney was one of the several fortifications constructed in the Tensaw region in the summer of 1813. Carney was a small stockade built on the property of a settler named Josiah Carney, located along the Tombigbee River a few miles north of Fort Powell. The recollections of one of its inhabitants, Margaret Eades (who later married Jeremiah Austill), have provided us with one of the most detailed accounts of life in the several settler stockades constructed during the Creek War.

The site of Fort Carney lies along the Tombigbee River in the vicinity of the area known as Carney's Bluff, a few miles south of Jackson, Alabama. It is unmarked.

Fort Cato

Fort Cato was one of the several fortifications constructed in the Tensaw region in the summer of 1813. Cato was a small stockade built on the property of one of the area's settlers on the west side of the Tombigbee River.

The site of Fort Cato lies in the area of the small community of Frankville in northeastern Washington County, Alabama. It is unmarked, and its exact location is unknown.

Fort Claiborne

Under orders from General Thomas Flournoy, General Ferdinand L. Claiborne constructed Fort Claiborne in November 1813. The fort, approximately two hundred feet square and featuring three blockhouses and a battery of artillery, was located along the Alabama River on a 150-foot-high limestone outcropping known as "Weatherford's Bluff." Flournoy originally intended the fort to serve as a supply depot for Andrew Jackson's troops, who at the time were believed to be preparing to march south to join Claiborne. From this location, Claiborne led a force of approximately one thousand men on a campaign against the Holy Ground in December 1813.

A historic plaque commemorating the fort stands on Highway 84 near its crossing of the Alabama River in Monroe County, Alabama.

Fort Deposit

General Ferdinand L. Claiborne's command constructed Fort Deposit in mid-December 1813 to serve as a supply depot during his campaign against the Holy Ground. Claiborne left his army's wagons, cannon and a small number of sick under the guard of approximately one hundred men here before setting out for the Creek village on December 22, 1813.

A view of the Alabama River from the site of Fort Claiborne. *Photo courtesy of authors.*

A historic marker commemorating the fort stands a short distance from its original location near Old Fort Road in Fort Deposit, Alabama. The fort site lies on private property.

Fort Easley (also known as Easley's Station)

The northernmost of the several forts constructed in the Tensaw region in the summer of 1813, Fort Easley was built on the property of a veteran of the Battle of Burnt Corn Creek. The fort was located on a bluff near the Tombigbee River about eight miles north of Fort Turner. It had been widely rumored that Fort Easley was to be a target of the Red Sticks in the weeks prior to the attack on Fort Mims. Responding to this threat, General Ferdinand Claiborne was at Easley when the massacre at Fort Mims occurred. Shortly afterward, the inhabitants of Fort Easley fled to the relative safety of St. Stephens.

The site of Fort Easley, presently unmarked, is located in the area known as Wood's Bluff, along the Tombigbee River in northwest Clarke County, Alabama.

Fort Deposit historical marker. *Photo courtesy of authors.*

Fort Glass

Fort Glass was built in July 1813 on the property of settler Zachariah Glass. It is believed to have enclosed an area of about sixty yards by forty yards. In September 1813, the fort's inhabitants fled to the more substantial Fort Madison, located only a few hundred yards away.

The site of Fort Glass lies near County Road 35 (Morning Star Road) near the community of Suggsville in southeastern Clarke County, Alabama. It is currently unmarked.

Fort Landrum

Fort Landrum was one of the several fortifications constructed in the Tensaw region in the summer of 1813. Landrum was a small stockade built on the property of one of the area's settlers a short distance from Fort Mott.

The site of Fort Landrum lies in the area of Salitpa Creek in central Clarke County, Alabama. It is unmarked, and its exact location is unknown.

Fort Lavier

Fort Lavier was one of the several fortifications constructed in the Tensaw region in the summer of 1813. Lavier was a small stockade built on the property of one of the area's settlers, and it is believed to have been located a few miles north of Fort Madison. Its residents fled to that stockade shortly after the fall of Fort Mims.

The site of Fort Lavier is believed to be in the vicinity of Bassett's Creek in central Clarke County, Alabama. It is unmarked, and its exact location is unknown.

Fort Madison

Reportedly named after President James Madison, Fort Madison was one of the more substantial of the several fortifications constructed in the Tensaw region in the summer of 1813. Troops under the command of Colonel Joseph Carson built the 60-square-yard stockade in August of that year about 225 yards away from the preexisting Fort Glass. Troops from Fort Madison were sent to bury the dead after the Kimbell-James massacre the next month, and the inhabitants of Fort Sinquefield fled to Madison after the attack on that stockade. Sometime prior to that, the people at Forts Glass and Lavier had also sought refuge at Madison. General Ferdinand Claiborne encouraged the inhabitants of Fort Madison to retreat to Fort Stoddert once he learned of what had happened at Sinquefield, and only a small number remained. One of these, Evans Austill, father of Jeremiah Austill, devised a way to light the perimeter of the fort by a tall pine torch that was kept ablaze at night.

The site of Fort Madison lies near County Road 35 (Morning Star Road) near the community of Suggsville in southeastern Clarke County,

Alabama. The fort is commemorated by a historic marker placed by the Daughters of the American Revolution in the early 1900s. A short distance away, on the opposite side of the road, lies the grave of Evans Austill.

Fort McGrew

Fort McGrew was one of several fortifications constructed in the Tensaw region in the summer of 1813. McGrew was a relatively large stockade, perhaps enclosing an area of up to two acres, built on the property of William and John McGrew along the Tombigbee River. The fort was located about three miles north of St. Stephens.

The site of Fort McGrew lies along the Tombigbee River in the area known as Little McGrew's Shoals, near the small community of Salitpa in southwestern Clarke County, Alabama. It is unmarked.

Fort Mims

Built around several structures on the plantation of prominent Tensaw District planter Samuel Mims, Fort Mims was the site of one of the greatest calamities in American military history. On August 30, 1813, a Red Stick force of seven hundred warriors attacked and destroyed the fort, both as a preemptory strike and as retaliation for being ambushed at Burnt Corn Creek a month earlier. Nearly 250 of the settlers, allied Creeks and members of the Mississippi territorial and local militias living in the one-acre facility at the time died during the day-long struggle. The news of the disaster jolted the nation and galvanized Americans in support of measures to put down the Red Stick rebellion.

Fort Mims Park, operated by the Alabama Historical Commission, is located at the original fort site just off County Road 80 in northwestern Baldwin County. The park features a partial reconstruction of the fort and interpretive signage that details the battle.

Fort Mott

Fort Mott was one of the several fortifications constructed in the Tensaw region in the summer of 1813. Mott was a small stockade built on the property of one of the area's settlers a short distance from Fort Landrum.

The site of Fort Mott lies in the area of Salitpa Creek in central Clarke County, Alabama. It is unmarked, and its exact location is unknown.

Reconstruction of Fort Mims. *Photo courtesy of authors.*

Fort Patton

Named in honor of its commander, James Patton, Fort Patton was a stockade constructed for the defense of settlers in Wayne County, Mississippi Territory, in the late summer of 1813. Settlers occupied the fort, located approximately seven miles south of Fort Roger, for only a short time before returning to their homes.

The site of Fort Patton lies within the community of Winchester, in Wayne County, Mississippi. The site of the fort is unmarked.

Fort Pierce

Named for brothers William and John Pierce, who operated a sawmill and gristmill on Pine Log Creek, Fort Pierce was one of several stockades erected by Tensaw district settlers in 1813. The fort was situated less than two miles southeast of Fort Mims, and those within it were able to clearly hear the battle that raged there on August 30, 1813. The next day, the fort's inhabitants fled to Mobile.

The site of the fort, located in northern Baldwin County, is currently unmarked and sits on private land.

Fort Pitchlynn (also known as Fort Smith)

Fort Pitchlynn is believed to have been constructed by the order of U.S. Interpreter for the Choctaws John Pitchlynn shortly after the outbreak of hostilities between American and Red Stick forces. The fort was utilized as a base of operations for Colonel John McKee in operations against Red Stick forces on the Black Warrior River. During this period, the fort became known as Fort Smith, probably named after Captain George Smith, an officer in McKee's command.

The site of the fort is located in the area known as Plymouth Bluff along the Tombigbee River in northwestern Lowndes County, Mississippi, just outside the city of Columbus. The Mississippi University for Women's Plymouth Bluff Center in Columbus contains exhibits detailing history of the area.

Fort Powell

Fort Powell was one of the several fortifications constructed in the Tensaw region in the summer of 1813. Powell was a small stockade built on the property of one of the area's settlers, located along the Tombigbee River a short distance south of Fort Carney.

The site of Fort Powell lies in the area known as Oven Bluff on the banks of the Tombigbee River, near the small community of Carlton in southern Clarke County, Alabama. It is unmarked.

Fort Rankin

Fort Rankin was the westernmost of the several fortifications constructed in the Tensaw region in the summer of 1813. Rankin was reputedly a large stockade built on the property of one of the area's settlers, located several miles west of the Tombigbee River and northwest of St. Stephens.

The site of Fort Rankin lies in north-central Washington County, Alabama. It is unmarked, and its exact location is unknown.

Fort Roger

Fort Roger was a stockade constructed for the defense of settlers in Wayne County, Mississippi Territory, in the late summer of 1813. Settlers occupied the fort, located approximately seven miles north of Fort Patton, for only a short time before returning to their homes.

The site of Fort Roger lies a short distance north of the community of Winchester, in Wayne County, Mississippi. It is unmarked, and its exact location is unknown.

Fort Sinquefield

Fort Sinquefield was one of the several fortifications constructed in the Tensaw region in the summer of 1813 and was home to approximately fifty settlers. A large group of Red Stick warriors attacked the fort on September 2, 1813, just as burial services were concluding for victims of the Kimbell and James families. Most of the people caught outside the fort's walls narrowly escaped to safety when a settler named Isaac Hayden famously turned a pack of hunting dogs on the attackers. In the two-hour battle, the fort's small garrison successfully held off the Red Stick force of several times their number. After the battle, the inhabitants of Fort Sinquefield fled to Fort Madison, ten miles south.

The site of Fort Sinquefield lies near Fort Sinquefield Road, a short distance off Highway 84 in the vicinity of the community of Whatley in central Clarke County, Alabama. The site is commemorated by a stone marker placed near the original site in 1931. About three quarters of a mile away, at the junction of Fort Sinquefield Road and Highway 84, is a more modern marker. About one mile east on Highway 84 stands a historic marker commemorating the Kimbell-James massacre.

Fort Stoddert

Named for Benjamin Stoddert, the first secretary of the U.S. Navy, Fort Stoddert was established in 1799 on the Mobile River near the boundary between the Mississippi Territory and Spanish West Florida. The fort was for a time a port of entry to United States territory, but it is most well known as the western terminus of the Federal Road connecting central Georgia with the Tensaw District. The fort, along with the nearby post at Mount Vernon, served as the central command center for military actions in the Tensaw region during the Creek War, as well as a place of refuge for settlers who fled the area in the wake of the attack on Fort Mims.

A historic marker commemorating Fort Stoddert stands alongside Highway 43 in the area of the modern communities of Mount Vernon and Fort Stoddard in northern Mobile County, Alabama. The actual fort site, now a landing on Mobile River, is located three miles east of the marker on County Road 96. It is unmarked.

Above: Fort Sinquefield monument. *Photo courtesy of authors.*

Right: Fort Stoddert historical marker. *Photo courtesy of authors.*

Fort Turner

Fort Turner was one of the several fortifications constructed in the Tensaw region in the summer of 1813. Turner featured a small stockade and is believed to have contained at least two blockhouses. Built on the property of a settler named Abner Turner, it was located about ten miles south of Fort Easley on the Tombigbee River. The inhabitants of Fort Turner fled for the relative safety of St. Stephens in the aftermath of the attack on Fort Mims.

The site of Fort Turner lies in the vicinity of the small community of West Bend in northwestern Clarke County, Alabama. It is unmarked, and its exact location is unknown. A few of the logs from the fort survive as part of a corncrib on display on the grounds of the Clarke County Museum in Grove Hill, Alabama.

Fort White

Fort White was one of the several fortifications constructed in the Tensaw region in the summer of 1813. White was a small stockade built on the property of one of the area's settlers a short distance from Fort Sinquefield.

The site of Fort White lies a few miles northeast of Grove Hill, Alabama. It is unmarked.

Hinson and Kennedy's Mills

Hinson and Kennedy's mills were prominent sawmills in the Tensaw District a few miles south of Fort Mims. They were major suppliers of lumber in their immediate area, as well as for work on the fortifications in Mobile and at Fort Bowyer on Mobile Point. Viewed as strategically important, the mills were protected by a stockade and garrisoned by a small detachment of troops. The site was abandoned shortly after the attack on Fort Mims and was later burned by Red Sticks.

A historic marker commemorating Kennedy's Mill stands on County Road 225 in northeastern Baldwin County, Alabama.

Holy Ground (Econochaca)

Holy Ground, a fortified town of over two hundred buildings, was located on a bluff in a curve of the Alabama River. Several Red Stick leaders lived there, and it also served as a base of supply and place of refuge for warriors during their struggle against the United States. According to the prophet Josiah Francis, the town had been rendered invincible to attack by whites through a magical ring of defense encircling it. The prophets believed that any white man who approached the town would instantly drop dead. Troops under the command of General Ferdinand L. Claiborne attacked and destroyed the town on December 23, 1813. During the fight, William Weatherford made a desperate escape by famously leaping his horse into the Alabama River.

The site of the Holy Ground lies in Holy Ground Battlefield Park in northern Lowndes County, Alabama, along the banks of the Alabama River. The park, which features interpretive signage containing information about the town and the battle, is located on Battlefield Road, a few miles north of Highway 80. At the junction of County Road 23 and Highway 80 stands a marker commemorating the battle.

Mount Vernon Cantonment

Mount Vernon, along with nearby Fort Stoddert on the banks of the Mobile River, served as the central command center for military actions in the Tensaw region during the Creek War. It was also a place of refuge for settlers who fled their homes in the wake of the attack on Fort Mims. The outpost at Mount Vernon had been constructed shortly before the outbreak of the Creek War approximately four miles west of Fort Stoddert in a supposedly more healthy location. The site later became the location of a federal arsenal, and it operated as a military post until the 1890s.

The site of the Mount Vernon Cantonment lies on the grounds of the Searcy Hospital in the modern community of Mount Vernon in northeastern Mobile County, Alabama. A historic marker interpreting the site's history as a federal arsenal stands along County Road 96 on the hospital grounds.

Randon's Creek (The Canoe Fight)

Randon's Creek is a tributary of the Alabama River in Monroe County, Alabama, named after a family who lived in the area at the time of the Creek War. The famous Canoe Fight occurred near the spot at which the creek empties into the Alabama, on the border between Monroe and Clarke Counties. On November 12, 1813, Sam Dale, Jeremiah Austill and James Smith, aboard a canoe paddled by a black man named Caesar, met and defeated in a brief but vicious fight a larger group of Red Stick warriors aboard another canoe in the middle of the river.

The exact location of the Canoe Fight is unknown and unmarked. A historic marker commemorating the event stands on County Road 35 (Morning Star Road) near the community of Suggsville in southeastern Clarke County, Alabama. A mural depicting the fight, painted by John Augustus Walker, is on display in Mobile's Old City Hall/Southern Market Complex, now the Museum of Mobile.

St. Stephens

St. Stephens was one of the principal settlements in the eastern portion of the Mississippi Territory, and it served at times as an administrative center for American military officials during the Creek War. The town was founded by the Spanish in the 1790s as a military outpost on a bluff overlooking the Tombigbee River. In 1799, the small settlement came under American control, and it was officially incorporated as a town in 1811. St. Stephens became the capital of the Alabama Territory in 1817 after the division of the Mississippi Territory following Mississippi's statehood.

The site of the town, long abandoned, lies within Old St. Stephens Historical Park, which is run by the St. Stephens Historical Commission. The park contains interpretive trails through the old streets of St. Stephens, cemeteries and a museum in the old Washington County Courthouse, among other recreational opportunities. The park is located off County Road 34 in northwest Washington County, Alabama.

Across the Chattahoochee

"For the first time, we heard to resound on the remote banks of the Tallapoosa the dreadful noise of contending armies, never before did the limpid waters receive the tinge of human blood."
— *Journal of James A. Tait for the year 1813*

In the wake of the attack on Fort Mims, the state of Georgia also moved to mobilize troops to put down the Red Stick rebellion. General John Floyd commanded the main Georgia army raised in response to the threat, composed of over twenty-three hundred volunteers and militia. Floyd hoped to advance his army into Creek Territory near the Coosa and Tallapoosa Rivers and join General Andrew Jackson's Tennessee force, eliminating resistance and constructing a series of fortified supply depots as it moved.

Floyd assembled his force—composed of two regiments of infantry, a battalion of riflemen and a company of artillery—at Fort Hawkins in Central Georgia in August and September 1813. Due to severe difficulties in obtaining supplies, Floyd's army did not march until late October. By that time, however, Floyd had learned of the Red Stick siege of the allied Creek town of Coweta on the banks of the Chattahoochee River. Allied Creeks based there had recently attacked a group of Red Sticks and raided several of their villages in the area, and Floyd considered it his first priority to relieve the town. By the time he advanced, sickness had reduced his army to only about 950 men. Following the Federal Road, the army made brief stops to construct Fort Lawrence and Fort Perry as it advanced west toward the Chattahoochee River. Upon his arrival at the Chattahoochee, Floyd learned that the siege of Coweta had been lifted.

His first objective already accomplished, Floyd moved a short distance downriver from the town and constructed Fort Mitchell to serve as the main supply base for his upcoming campaign. After being reinforced by over three hundred allied Creeks led by William McIntosh, Floyd's

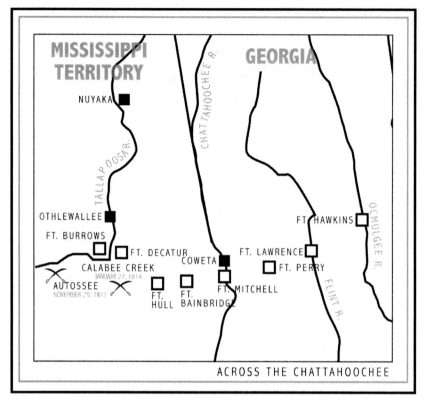

Map by Jessica McCarty.

army set out for the Red Stick village of Autossee, a significant Red Stick population and military center on the Tallapoosa River. It may also have been the home of some of the warriors who attacked Fort Mims. Floyd's army, guided by a local trader, reached the town on November 29.

Floyd divided his army into two columns to encircle the town, placing the commands of Lieutenant Colonel David S. Booth and Captain William E. Adams on the right and those of Lieutenant Colonel James C. Watson and Captain James Meriwether on the left. He ordered McIntosh's allied Creeks to cross the Tallapoosa to prevent the retreat of the Red Sticks. The unexpected discovery of another town (in actuality, this "town" was another part of Autossee) only a few hundred yards from Autossee, however, disrupted Floyd's plans. Forced to include the other town in the planned encirclement, Floyd's lines were stretched too thin to accomplish the maneuver. The Red Sticks discovered Floyd's approach, evacuated noncombatants and braced themselves for the assault.

The battle began about daybreak on a bitterly cold, frosty morning. Coosa Miko, the ranking Red Stick leader in the town at the time, ordered his men to wait until Floyd's troops were almost upon them before he gave the order to fire. After the opening volley, they charged the Georgians, but the fire of two artillery pieces repulsed their attack. Floyd's troops then countercharged the Red Sticks, driving them into Autossee and the nearby woods. An intense firefight ensued, during which the Red Sticks suffered heavy casualties. Many were shot as they tried to escape across the Tallapoosa, and many others were burned in their houses as the village became engulfed in flames. At the other town on Floyd's left, the Georgians quickly overtook the defenders and forced their retreat. With the Tallapoosa swollen from recent heavy rains, McIntosh's troops had been unable to cross the river and instead attempted to prevent retreat across nearby Calabee Creek. Despite their efforts, the majority of the Red Sticks escaped.

The fighting concluded by midmorning. About two hundred Red Sticks lay dead, with the American forces suffering only eleven killed and approximately fifty wounded. Significant leaders of both armies were among the casualties. General Floyd was severely wounded by a musket

"The Georgia Militia under General Floyd attacking the Creek Indians at Autossee." *Courtesy of the Hargrett Rare Book and Manuscript Library/University of Georgia Libraries.*

ball in the knee, while Coosa Miko suffered both gunshot and saber wounds. While Coosa Miko managed to escape, Hopoithle Miko, one of the most outspoken and revered Red Stick leaders, died in the battle after being struck by cannon fire.

Though he had destroyed one of the principal Red Stick towns, Floyd could not follow up on his victory. A severe shortage of supplies forced Floyd to march his army back to Fort Mitchell. After he left, another group of Red Sticks led by Paddy Walsh—who had been summoned earlier in the day, but had not arrived in time to take part in the battle—attacked and drove off a group of McIntosh's allied Creeks who had stayed behind. Walsh pursued Floyd's army, attacking it in a brief skirmish after it had paused to bury its dead. Despite Walsh's efforts, Floyd's army reached Fort Mitchell safely a few days later.

Floyd's retreat occurred simultaneously with another offensive by Georgia troops that targeted the territory immediately north of the Autossee area. Major General Thomas Pinckney, commander of the Sixth Military District and thus in overall command of the campaigns, selected Major General David Adams to lead this second expedition into Red Stick territory. Adams departed from Monticello, Georgia, with over five hundred troops in early December, targeting Creek towns on the Tallapoosa River. The army fought a few minor skirmishes with Red Sticks before arriving at the town of Nuyaka in mid-December. Discovering the town abandoned, Adams ordered it burned, and his army retraced its steps back to Georgia.

After regrouping and building up a store of supplies, Floyd's army took the field again in January 1814 with approximately fifteen hundred men—eleven hundred militia and several hundred allied Creeks. Floyd now targeted Othlewallee, a Creek town on the Tallapoosa where William Weatherford, Paddy Walsh, High Head Jim, William McGillivray and other Red Stick leaders had gathered to plot strategy. The army built Fort Hull about forty miles west of Fort Mitchell to serve as its supply base for the operation. A few days later, as they advanced toward the Tallapoosa River, the army paused to construct a fortified camp near Calabee Creek. The location was later dubbed Camp Defiance.

Aware of Floyd's approach, the Red Stick leaders at Othlewallee plotted a surprise attack. After a disagreement over the best way to attack Floyd's army, William Weatherford allegedly left the area angrily and Paddy Walsh assumed overall command of the attack plans. In perhaps the best-planned Red Stick attack of the war, approximately thirteen hundred

"The Battle of Calabee Creek," by John Gardner. *Courtesy of John Gardner.*

warriors fell upon Camp Defiance in the early morning hours of January 27, 1814. Although Floyd's men built campfires on the perimeter of the camp as a defense mechanism against a surprise attack, the assault nearly overwhelmed the American position. A portion of Floyd's command even became separated from the main army and might have been destroyed had it not been for the quick action of Timpoochee Barnard and his small band of allied warriors. It took Floyd's two artillery pieces to slow the Red Stick onslaught. These two cannon were a prime objective of the Red Stick attack, and some of the most vicious fighting in the battle took place in the attempt to capture the guns. After a countercharge by the American troops, the Red Sticks, many of whom were poorly armed or running out of ammunition, withdrew shortly after daybreak.

After the Battle of Calabee Creek, nearly 50 Red Sticks, including the leader Jim Boy, lay dead. Casualties in Floyd's army included 22 whites and allied Creeks killed and nearly 150 wounded. The army remained at Camp Defiance about a week before moving back toward Fort Hull. With their terms of enlistment about to expire, Floyd marched the majority of his troops back to Georgia for discharge and left Colonel Homer V. Milton with 140 volunteers in command at Fort Hull.

Reinforcements ordered from the Carolinas by General Pinckney arrived at Fort Hull shortly after Floyd left for Georgia. Milton quickly employed them in the construction of Fort Bainbridge, about fifteen miles east from Hull, to protect the tenuous supply line from Fort Mitchell. Milton

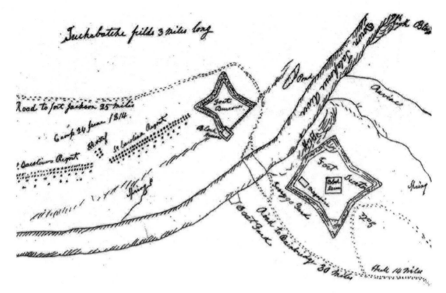

Map showing the location of Fort Burrows and Fort Decatur. *Copy courtesy of James Walker and Family and Glenn Drummond.*

continued to strengthen these positions throughout March 1814 and constructed two other fortifications—Fort Decatur and Fort Burrows along the Tallapoosa River—in April. Following the Battle of Horseshoe Bend, Milton moved his command to the Hickory Ground and united with the army of General Andrew Jackson to build Fort Jackson near the confluence of the Coosa and Tallapoosa Rivers. Milton ultimately ended the war at Fort Claiborne, where he had gone in support of operations to eliminate the remaining scattered pockets of Red Stick resistance.

Historic Sites

Autossee (Atasi)

Located on the banks of the Tallapoosa River in present-day Macon County, Alabama, Autossee was one of the largest Red Stick towns. A village of at least two hundred houses, the town's name literally meant "War Club." It was home to some of the most vocal Red Stick leaders, including High Head Jim, and may have been the home of some of the warriors that attacked Fort Mims. Troops under the command of General John Floyd destroyed the town during the battle on November 29, 1813.

Site of the Battle of Autossee. *Photo courtesy of authors.*

The site of the town today lies on private property near Shorter, in northwestern Macon County, Alabama, and is unmarked and inaccessible to the public.

Camp Defiance (The Battle of Calabee Creek)

Troops under the command of General John Floyd constructed Camp Defiance in January 1814 as they made their second advance into Creek territory. In the Battle of Calabee Creek, Red Stick forces attacked and nearly routed the camp in the predawn darkness of January 27, 1814.

The camp was located near the confluence of Calebee Creek and the Tallapoosa River in present-day northwestern Macon County, Alabama, near County Road 73. It lies on private land, and there is currently no marker commemorating the site.

Coweta

An allied Creek town, Coweta was a major Creek population and political center in the Chattahoochee Valley region and home to several influential allied Creek leaders, most notably William McIntosh. Red Stick forces besieged the town in the fall of 1813.

The town was located on the western bank of the Chattahoochee River a few miles south of modern-day Phenix City, Alabama. A historical marker commemorating the town stands near its location on Brickyard Road.

Fort Bainbridge

Fort Bainbridge was constructed by troops under the command of Colonel Homer V. Milton in January 1814 to help protect the supply line connecting Fort Hull and Fort Mitchell. The fort is believed to have been named in honor of naval captain William Bainbridge.

The fort was located in present-day Macon County, Alabama, near the boundary with Russell County. It is unmarked.

Fort Burrows

Fort Burrows was a small fortification built in the spring of 1814 on the banks of the Tallapoosa River opposite of Fort Decatur.

The site of Fort Burrows lies in southeastern Elmore County, Alabama, across the Tallapoosa River from the E.V. Smith Research Center in Macon County, Alabama. It is unmarked and lies on private land.

Fort Daniel

Fort Daniel was constructed in 1813 and garrisoned by the Twenty-fifth Regiment of the Georgia Militia. The fort is believed to have been named for General Allen Daniel, a leading politician and militia commander.

The fort is commemorated by a historic marker located north of Lawrenceville, Georgia, in Gwinnett County, near the intersection of Georgia State Highway 124 and Georgia State Highway 324.

Fort Decatur

Colonel Homer V. Milton ordered the construction of Fort Decatur, located on the banks of the Tallapoosa River near the Creek village of Tuckaubatchee, to serve as a base of supply in April 1814. The fort is believed to have been named in honor of naval hero Stephen Decatur Jr. The fort remained garrisoned for the duration of the war, and

Remnants of the earthen walls of Fort Decatur. *Photo courtesy of authors.*

subsequently became the meeting place for representatives of the United States Boundary Commission, which had been appointed to survey the new boundary between Creek territory and the state of Georgia.

The fort site is marked by a stone marker placed by the Alabama Anthropological Society in 1931. An iron fence—originally placed around the grave of John Sevier, chairman of the boundary commission, who died at the fort in 1815—surrounds the marker. The site is located on the grounds of Auburn University's E.V. Smith Research Center near Milstead, Alabama. It is open to the public with prior permission of the staff of the research center.

Fort Hawkins

The United States government ordered the construction of Fort Hawkins in 1806 after the Treaty of Washington established the Ocmulgee River as the boundary with the Creek Nation. Named for Indian Agent Benjamin Hawkins, the fort was located along the river near a group of Indian mounds. During the war, the fort served as a gathering spot for

Reconstruction of the Fort Hawkins blockhouse. *Photo courtesy of authors.*

troops sent to fight both the Red Stick Creeks and the British along the Gulf Coast.

The fort site is located in Macon, Georgia, on Fort Hill Street adjacent to the Ocmulgee National Monument. The site, which contains a reproduction of one of the fort's two blockhouses, stands on the location of the original structure and is maintained by the city. It is open to the public, but appointments are necessary.

Fort Hull

Fort Hull was constructed to serve as a supply base by General John Floyd's army on its second expedition into Creek territory in January

1814. Following the fort's construction, Floyd's army moved toward the Tallapoosa River, leaving its baggage and wagons behind shortly before the Battle of Calabee Creek. Following Floyd's retreat to Georgia, Colonel Homer V. Milton assumed command of the post with a small number of volunteers and awaited reinforcements from the Carolinas. From this base of operations, he oversaw construction of nearby Fort Bainbridge.

The fort site is currently unmarked and is located on private property off County Road 45 in central Macon County, Alabama.

Fort Lawrence

Located on the banks of the Flint River, Fort Lawrence was constructed by General John Floyd's troops in November 1813 as they made their way from Fort Hawkins into Creek Territory.

The fort site is located in present-day eastern Taylor County, Georgia, along the banks of the Flint River. It is not marked, and its exact location is unknown.

Fort Mitchell

General John Floyd ordered the construction of Fort Mitchell in November 1813 to serve as a base of supply for his expedition into Creek territory. Named in honor of Georgia Governor David Mitchell, the fort featured two blockhouses and several supporting structures. Floyd's army regrouped at Fort Mitchell between its sorties into Creek territory and the resulting battles at Autossee and Calabee Creek. The fort continued to play a major role in relations between the United States and the Creeks after the war, becoming the location of the Creek Trading Factory and the Creek Indian Agency. Rebuilt in 1825, the fort was subsequently visited by several notable figures, including the Marquis de Lafayette, General Winfield Scott and Francis Scott Key. Fort Mitchell continued in service until the conclusion of the Second Creek War, when it became a gathering place for Creeks to be removed west.

Today, a reconstruction of the fort stands near its original location, in Fort Mitchell National Landmark Site on Highway 431 a few miles south of Phenix City, Alabama.

Reconstruction of Fort Mitchell. *Photo courtesy of authors.*

Fort Peachtree

Fort Peachtree was built in the spring of 1814 at the junction of Peachtree Creek and the Chattahoochee River near a Cherokee village known as Standing Peach Tree. Lieutenant George Gilmer oversaw its construction. General Thomas Pinckney intended the fort to serve as a supply depot for American forces during the Creek War. The war ended, however, before the fort could be used to significantly assist American military operations.

A reconstruction of the fort, located in the Buckhead area of Atlanta, Georgia, near a waterworks facility, stands on the original location of the structure today. A historic marker is located on the site as well. The site is restricted, but it is open to the public with permission from the city.

Fort Perry

Troops under the command of General John Floyd began Fort Perry, located along the Federal Road halfway between Fort Lawrence on the

Flint River and Fort Mitchell on the Chattahoochee, in the fall of 1813 on their way to Creek Territory. The fort was named for Oliver Hazard Perry, a hero of the Battle of Lake Erie. The wooden stockade featured two blockhouses and was garrisoned for only a few months. The fort is believed to have been star shaped rather than rectangular because of the presence of a shallow, sixteen-sided ditch on the site.

Fort Perry is marked by a historical marker about ten miles north of Buena Vista in Marion County, Georgia, on Georgia Highway 41. The actual fort site is a short distance away on private property.

Nuyaka (New Yaucau)

Nuyaka was a Creek town of approximately eighty houses located on the Tallapoosa River opposite the village of Tohopeka. The town's residents abandoned Nuyaka in the fall of 1813 shortly before troops under the command of Major General David Adams destroyed it in December 1813. Nuyaka received its name from the 1790 Treaty of New York, negotiated between Creek leaders and the United States government, in which the Creeks ceded a portion of their lands in the current state of Georgia to the United States.

The site of the town is today located within the boundaries of the Horseshoe Bend National Military Park, across the Tallapoosa River from the Horseshoe Bend battlefield.

Othlewallee

Located on the Tallapoosa River near Autossee, Othlewallee was a major Red Stick settlement. A spiritual headquarters and strategic gathering spot for Red Stick leaders similar to the Holy Ground on the Alabama River, Othlewallee was home to as many as five hundred warriors. General John Floyd targeted the town on his second campaign into Creek territory. William Weatherford, Paddy Walsh and other leaders plotted the surprise attack on Camp Defiance here.

The site of Othlewallee lies on the banks of the Tallapoosa River in present-day Elmore County, Alabama. It is unmarked.

The Path to Horseshoe Bend

"We have retaliated for the destruction of Fort Mims...if we had a sufficient supply of provisions we should in a very short time, accomplish the object of the expedition."
—*General Andrew Jackson to Governor Willie Blount following the Battle of Tallushatchee, November 4, 1813*

News of the Fort Mims massacre both saddened and pleased Andrew Jackson. He hated to read about the deaths of so many soldiers and civilians, but he rejoiced that the United States would finally be able to enter the war. The foremost spokesman for the interests of the West, Jackson saw in the massacre of Fort Mims an opportunity to eliminate European influence on the Gulf Coast and acquire from the Creeks valuable land for the growing country. He gladly complied when Tennessee Governor Willie Blount asked him to command a force of militia to put down the Creek rebellion. Volunteers and militia were soon mobilized with orders to rendezvous at Fayetteville in early October.

Jackson had already acquired a military reputation in the War of 1812. In early 1813, he led a force of Tennesseans to Natchez in the Mississippi Territory to take part in the defense of the Gulf Coast. His dreams of early glory were quickly dashed, however, when his men were dismissed before seeing action. Jackson swallowed his pride and led his men back to Tennessee via a long, exhausting march up the Natchez Trace to Nashville. He earned the respect of his troops as he suffered alongside them on the march, and they began to call him "Old Hickory" for his toughness. On his second entry into the war, Jackson would live up to that nickname and more.

Jackson commanded one of two forces of Tennessee militia sent in response to the attack on Fort Mims. His command consisted of an army

Map by Jessica McCarty.

of one thousand militia and volunteers and thirteen hundred cavalrymen under the leadership of his friend and confidant John Coffee. An East Tennessee unit of twenty-five hundred men, under the overall command of John Cocke, was to cooperate with Jackson's command. In addition, hundreds of allied Creeks, Choctaws and Cherokees would eventually assist these Tennesseans, many of whom wore white plumes in their hats to distinguish them from their foes. As these forces advanced into Creek territory, they planned to build roads, establish supply depots and destroy Red Stick resistance.

Jackson arrived at Camp Blount in Fayetteville on October 7. Coffee's cavalry had already been sent southward, and now Jackson followed them with his army. Moving an incredible thirty miles a day, the army crossed the Tennessee River at Ditto's Landing and established Fort Deposit by October 22. Jackson hoped supplies would be forthcoming. Keeping his men fed would prove to be a harder task than defeating the Red Sticks.

Jackson soon learned of an enemy village at Tallushatchee and sent Coffee to destroy it while he moved the remainder of his command to Ten Islands on the Coosa River and established Fort Strother. Splitting his men into two columns on his approach to Tallushatchee on November 3, 1813, Coffee surrounded the town and lured the Red Stick warriors into the mainline. The engagement was more a massacre than a battle. In only thirty minutes, Coffee's troops killed almost two hundred Red Sticks, causing Tennessee volunteer David Crockett to remark afterward that "we shot them like dogs." Thrilled with this first American victory of the war, Jackson informed Governor Blount that he had retaliated for the attack on Fort Mims.

The Battle of Tallushatchee would have a profound impact on Jackson personally as well as professionally. After the fight, American troops found an infant Creek boy and brought him to Jackson. The general felt a kinship to this orphan child due to his own scarred childhood and sent him to his wife to be raised in their home. Lyncoya, as he became known, lived with the Jacksons until his death shortly before his seventeenth birthday.

While at Fort Strother, Jackson received a plea for help from the nearby friendly Creek village of Talladega. Typifying the civil war aspect of the conflict, over 1,000 Red Sticks under the command of William Weatherford laid siege to about 150 Creeks huddled in a small fort. Jackson wanted to move immediately to their aid, but he had concerns due to his number of sick and wounded. Jackson still hoped to be reinforced and resupplied by Cocke, whose advance force led by James White marched from Knoxville toward a rendezvous with Jackson's army. White's men had recently paused on their trek to construct Fort Armstrong at the junction of the Coosa and Chattooga Rivers with the help of allied Cherokees. A political rival of Jackson, Cocke feared that combining his men with Old Hickory would prevent him from achieving the glory he craved, and therefore, he decided to recall White back to Fort Armstrong.

Though unsure of the reason for Cocke's delay, Jackson took the risk and proceeded to relieve Talladega. On November 9, 1813, using the same plan that Coffee had used at Tallushatchee, he attempted to encircle the Red Sticks and then lure them into a trap with a feint. His plan worked perfectly. Jackson's men shot down the Red Sticks in droves in the battle, but a failure to complete the encirclement allowed nearly seven hundred to escape. Although furious over the failure to completely annihilate the Red Sticks, Jackson had won a smashing victory. His men had killed over three hundred Red Sticks at a cost of fewer than one hundred casualties. He still had not made contact with Cocke, however, and a lack of supplies forced him to retreat back to Fort Strother. Had Jackson's men been able to pursue the weakened and disorganized Red Sticks at this point, he might have won the Creek War much earlier.

The battle at Talladega had some unintended and far-reaching consequences on the course of the war. In the aftermath of the battle, several Red Stick towns decided that they had had enough and wanted peace. Warriors from the Hillabee towns even sent word to Jackson that they wanted to surrender. Unfortunately, Cocke had already sent his advance force under White toward the area before Jackson could inform him of the proposed surrender. White's men destroyed several towns between November 11 and 17, and on November 18, they attacked the main Hillabee town. In the attack, largely conducted by a contingent of Cherokee allies, approximately 70 inhabitants were killed and over 250 were taken prisoner. Members of the Hillabee towns never forgave this "betrayal," and many would later fight to the death at Horseshoe Bend.

The months following the Battle of Talladega challenged Jackson as he struggled to keep his volunteer army supplied and intact. Shortly after the army's return to Fort Strother, members of his militia, whose terms of enlistment were about to expire, decided to return home. Jackson used his volunteers to prevent them from leaving. Ironically, the next day, the situation reversed as Jackson used his militia to prevent his volunteers from attempting to return home.

Jackson continued to plead for his men to stay and assured them that the desperately needed supplies would soon arrive, but he ultimately decided to march the majority of his men back to Fort Deposit. After he had managed to gather enough volunteers to hold the fort, he marched the remainder of his army northward. They soon encountered the

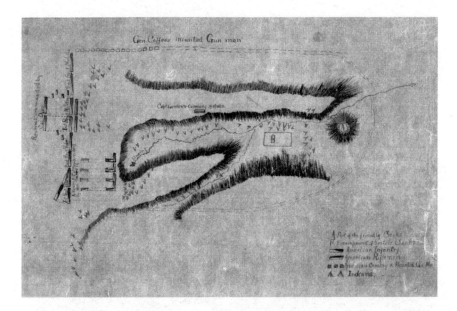

A map of the Battle of Talladega. *Courtesy of the Alabama Department of Archives and History.*

much-anticipated supply wagons and for the first time in weeks enjoyed an adequate meal. When the troops attempted to continue marching toward home rather than return to Fort Strother, Jackson, angered at their lack of resolve, grabbed a musket and personally threatened to shoot the first solider who attempted to desert. Intimidated by Jackson's determination, the troops reluctantly marched back to Fort Strother.

Despite Jackson's attempts to maintain order, which even included aiming cannon at his men at one point, most of his men left after their enlistments expired. Cocke's troops' tardy arrival in December failed to alleviate the problem since their enlistments expired soon as well. Even Coffee's cavalry, long a source of pride to Jackson, deserted while they foraged for food for their horses near Huntsville. Eventually, barely over one hundred men remained with Jackson at Fort Strother.

The situation improved in mid-January 1814 when over eight hundred new troops finally arrived. Jackson decided to move forward immediately. He had heard rumors of an anticipated British landing in Florida, and he wanted to eliminate the Red Stick threat before they could join forces with the British. Just as importantly, Jackson wanted to utilize these new volunteers before their brief terms of enlistment expired. With his force of about one thousand men, he moved southward toward the Tallapoosa

"Andrew Jackson Quelling the Mutiny." *Courtesy of the Library of Congress.*

River, where he hoped to destroy a Red Stick force at the village of Tohopeka. For the only time in the Creek War, Jackson launched an offensive in which he would be outnumbered by his opponent. His men moved quickly and encamped within three miles of the enemy at Emuckfau Creek. His scouts informed him that the Red Sticks were aware of their presence, so Jackson prepared for their assault.

Before dawn on January 22, 1814, nearly one thousand Red Sticks attacked the encampment. Successfully repelling the initial onslaught, Jackson sent Coffee's cavalry forward to determine the feasibility of an attack on Tohopeka. Coffee found the village strongly fortified and informed Jackson that it would not be simple to capture. Coffee had barely reported this news when the Red Sticks launched yet another attack. This time, the onslaught threatened the encampment from all sides. The attackers skillfully fired from trees, brush and anything else that could provide cover. It took a charge by Coffee's men, in which Coffee sustained serious injuries, to finally stagger the Creek attack. Red Stick leader Peter McQueen had planned a third assault, but this fell apart when some of the warriors abandoned him and left for home—a situation with which Jackson himself could sympathize.

Jackson had won a victory at Emuckfau Creek, but he knew better than to push his luck and decided to march his army back to Fort Strother. Satisfied that he had learned what he needed about the stronghold at Tohopeka, Jackson hoped that his foray had at least taken pressure off John Floyd's Georgia troops who were on a campaign nearby. Unfortunately for Jackson and his men, the Red Sticks would not let his men retreat in peace.

On January 24, the Red Sticks attacked again as the army crossed Enitachopco Creek. Jackson hoped to use his rear guard to contain the attack and to use his favorite tactic of taking the remainder of his troops to encircle the enemy army. To his dismay, however, the war cries of the Red Sticks panicked his rear guard and many of them dashed away. The attackers made a concerted effort to capture Jackson's artillery piece during the fight, but Old Hickory himself aided his brave artillerists as they barely fought off the attacks. Finally driving off the Red Sticks, Jackson's men continued their retreat to Fort Strother. Despite being taken by surprise on two occasions, Jackson's army had suffered fewer than one hundred casualties while inflicting close to double that number.

As he began the task of revitalizing his army, Jackson learned that his successes and determination had impressed his commanding officer,

Major General Thomas Pinckney. Pinckney, who led the Sixth Military District and had been placed in charge of the entire Creek War effort, decided that Jackson was the man to win this war and sent him the U.S. Thirty-ninth Regiment, a force of regulars that Jackson had long coveted. Major Lemuel Montgomery and a third lieutenant by the name of Sam Houston were included in this detachment. Under the command of Colonel John Williams, the unit arrived at Fort Strother on February 6. Jackson also received new Tennessee volunteers, who were rushed to him from Governor Blount, a force of one hundred allied Creeks led by William McIntosh and nearly five hundred Cherokees led by a chief known as Ridge, who would later take "Major" as his first name. These troops swelled the army to over five thousand men.

Jackson spent most of the months of February and March 1814 training and disciplining the army that would ultimately break the power of the Red Sticks. As part of their daily training, he also had the troops improve the road from Fort Deposit to Fort Strother. While supplies steadily poured in, Jackson made plans for another offensive on Tohopeka.

The army marched out on March 14. Jackson paused on the banks of the Coosa to build a supply base—named Fort Williams in honor

Diorama of the Battle of Horseshoe Bend. *Courtesy of the National Park Service.*

The village of Tohopeka. *Courtesy of the National Park Service.*

of the leader of the Thirty-ninth Regiment—at a place called Three Islands. Continuing its march, the army arrived near Tohopeka on March 27. Located in a bend of the Tallapoosa, the Creeks called the one-hundred-acre plot of land *Cholocco Litabixee,* or "the horse's flat foot," but the Americans simply called it Horseshoe Bend. One thousand warriors under Menewa awaited Jackson behind an impressive fortification that spanned 350 yards across the neck of land in the curve of the river. The barricade consisted of logs stacked five to eight feet high and situated in a way that subjected attackers to crossfire. Though formidable, Jackson saw that the Creeks had trapped themselves behind their fortification. He dispatched Coffee along with his Native American allies to the opposite side of the river to block their only avenue of escape and made plans for his attack.

Jackson began the decisive battle at 10:30 a.m. with an artillery bombardment. With the Red Sticks screaming defiance, his artillery poured shots into their barricade. During the bombardment, Coffee and his Native American allies entered the fight. Several Cherokees crossed the river, captured the Red Sticks' canoes to prevent them from being used to escape and then pressed on into the village, eventually setting it on fire.

Aerial view of Horseshoe Bend. *Courtesy of the National Park Service.*

When Jackson saw the smoke from the fires of Tohopeka and realized the ineffectiveness of the artillery bombardment, he ordered an all-out frontal assault. Regulars from the Thirty-ninth Regiment spearheaded the attack, joined by one brigade of the Tennessee militia. The soldiers charged energetically and scaled the fortifications in a matter of minutes. Major Montgomery was one of the first over the wall, but he was shot in the head and killed instantly. Sam Houston was also wounded in the initial assault, but he continued onward, only to suffer additional wounds later in the fighting.

Once the barricade had been breached, the battle turned into a slaughter in which more Native Americans would die than in any other battle in North American history. The Red Sticks fought defiantly, but being assailed on both sides by superior numbers sealed their doom. Many tried to escape by swimming the river, but Coffee's men mowed them down. Red Sticks who tried to hide were also quickly found and killed. Three Red Stick prophets were among the casualties, but Menewa managed to escape that night despite being wounded seven times. Jackson's men counted over 550 Red Stick bodies on the field after the battle, and officers estimated the total killed to be upwards

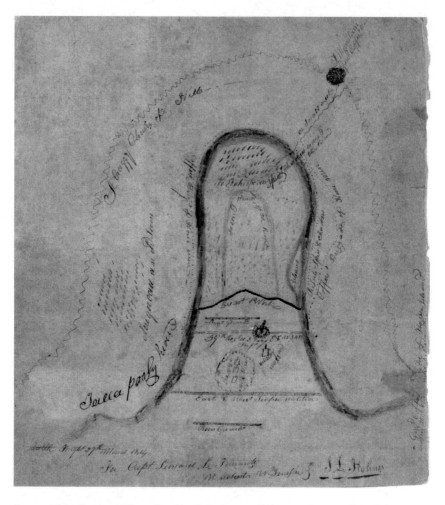

A map of the Battle of Horseshoe Bend, by Leonard Tarrant. *Courtesy of the Alabama Department of Archives and History.*

of 900. Jackson's army, on the other hand, had less than 50 killed and about 150 wounded.

In the aftermath of the battle, Jackson allegedly ordered his men to cut off the tips of the noses of the dead Red Sticks to ensure an accurate count of their casualties. Many soldiers went even further, celebrating the victory by cutting long bands of skin off dead Red Sticks to make trophies such as belts and bridle reins. Though scattered pockets of Red Stick resistance remained to be eliminated, their power had been shattered.

Jackson did not know the extent of his triumph at the time, however, and he moved his army back to Fort Williams to resupply and prepare for another campaign. He now targeted the Hickory Ground at the confluence of the Coosa and Tallapoosa Rivers, an area known to be a major gathering spot for hostiles. Jackson marched his force southward on April 5, destroying hostile Creek villages and food supplies as he moved. On April 17, he arrived at the site of the old French Fort Toulouse, which had been designated as the gathering point for his army along with troops from Georgia, South Carolina, North Carolina and the Mississippi Territory. Soldiers built a stockade on the site and named it Fort Jackson.

Soon, hundreds of starving Creek refugees, many of them allies, made their way into the army's encampment. Jackson sent them northward to the rear of his own army around Fort Williams to settle, thereby hopefully removing them from any possible British or Spanish influence. The bulk of the remaining Red Sticks had already fled southward, looking for aid from European allies. One day, William Weatherford, the principal Red Stick leader whose surrender Jackson especially desired, walked into camp alone and surrendered himself to Jackson. "I am in your power," legend has him saying to the general. "Once I could animate my warriors to battle, but I can not animate the dead...their bones are at Talladega,

"Interview Between General Jackson and Weatherford." *Courtesy of the Library of Congress.*

Tallushatchee, Emuckfau and Tohopeka." Although many called for Jackson to have Weatherford executed, the Red Stick leader's courage impressed Old Hickory. Jackson decided to let Weatherford go on his vow that he would no longer raise arms against the United States and that he would do everything in his power to encourage the remaining Red Sticks to surrender. Weatherford followed through with Jackson's request and eventually returned to his life as a planter.

As refugees continued to pour into the camp, it soon became obvious to all that the war was indeed over. General Thomas Pinckney soon arrived at Fort Jackson and directed Old Hickory to march his men home. Along the way, Jackson stopped several times to issue addresses to his men, thanking them for their service. At Fort Williams, he told them that they had "annihilated the power of a nation, that, for twenty years, has been the disturber of peace. Your vengeance has been glutted."

Tennesseans greeted Jackson as a hero on his return to Nashville. At a time when the War of 1812 was going badly for the country, he had destroyed his enemy on the battlefield and earned the respect and admiration of the nation. The War Department acknowledged his hard-earned status as the country's foremost military leader by offering him a major generalship. On June 18, 1814, Jackson became a major general in the U.S. Army, responsible for the Seventh Military District comprising Louisiana, Tennessee, the Mississippi Territory and the Creek Nation.

A daunting task awaited him. Prior to his promotion, Secretary of War John Armstrong had assigned Pinckney and Creek Indian Agent Benjamin Hawkins to negotiate the peace treaty with the Creeks. Armstrong instructed them to ask the Creeks for an indemnity of the cost of the war, require a stoppage in trade and communication with the British and Spanish, allow the United States to build roads and forts through the territory and turn over any surviving prophets and Red Stick instigators of war. Armstrong ordered Jackson to report to Fort Jackson and assume control of treaty negotiations himself.

Jackson heavily influenced the final terms of the treaty. An advocate for land-hungry Westerners, he expected the Creeks to pay dearly for the war. Since Jackson also wanted to remove the Creeks from contact with the Spanish and British, he viewed forcibly removing the Creeks from the region as a necessity. Altruistically, he felt the Creek way of life was so incompatible with that of whites that removal was the only way for them to survive. Upon arrival, Jackson called a meeting of all Creek chiefs on August 1 to begin a new round of negotiations. Old Hickory's

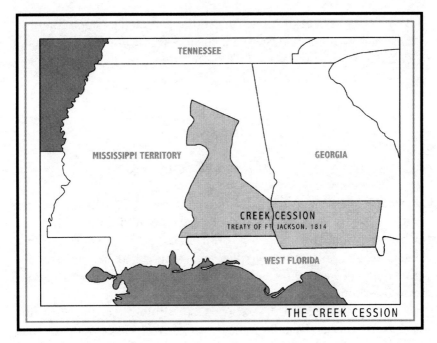

Map by Jessica McCarty.

terms were much harsher than those previously offered by Pinckney and Hawkins. He required the cession of twenty-three million acres of land, half of all Creek territory, to the United States. This land amounted to almost three-fifths of the future state of Alabama and one-fifth of Georgia. Jackson also insisted on the other original requirements of the treaty, including ceasing all interaction with the British and Spanish. If the Creeks refused these terms, then they could take their chances and simply move southward and join the rebels in Florida.

Jackson's terms shocked the allied Creeks in attendance. They expected only the Red Sticks to bear the brunt of the cost of the war. While they expected to lose some land, they did not expect their ally to repay them in this way for their service. They pleaded with Jackson about the fairness of his terms, but to no avail. Jackson chastised all the Creeks for allowing the war to occur. He claimed that they should have arrested Tecumseh and other instigators and prophets immediately. The Creeks had no choice but to sign the Treaty of Fort Jackson on August 9, 1814. Ironically, of the nearly three dozen chiefs that signed on behalf of the Creeks, only one is believed to have been a Red Stick. Henceforward, Jackson would become known by the Creeks as "Sharp Knife" for his harshness.

The Treaty of Fort Jackson signaled the end of the Creek Nation as a military power, but Red Sticks remained a threat to the United States. Events developing on the Gulf Coast revealed that threat and led to a new, and final, stage in the conflict.

Historic Sites

Buckhorn Tavern

Located north of Huntsville, this tavern served as a stop for pioneers as they traveled throughout the region. A portion of Andrew Jackson's supply route ran from here to Fort Deposit on the Tennessee River. John Coffee's cavalry stored supplies and camped here in late 1813. The structure earned its nickname in the late 1850s after a hunter presented a set of deer antlers to the tavern's owner.

The original building no longer exists, but a historic marker interpreting the tavern is located at the intersection of Winchester and Maysfield Road north of Huntsville.

Site of Camp Blount. *Photo courtesy of authors.*

Camp Blount (Fayetteville, TN)

After the massacre at Fort Mims, Tennessee militia met at Camp Blount in Fayetteville, Tennessee, to prepare for action against the Red Sticks. Andrew Jackson joined them in October 1813 at this camp, named after Governor Willie Blount, to take command and begin the march southward.

The site is located in downtown Fayetteville on Huntsville Highway (Highway 431/231) and is marked with a historic marker near a few ancient oak trees.

Ditto's Landing

Troops under Andrew Jackson crossed the Tennessee River here as they advanced southward against the Red Stick Creeks.

The crossing site is located on the grounds of the Ditto's Landing (Huntsville-Madison County) Marina along the banks of the Tennessee River on Highway 231, south of Huntsville, Alabama. The site, however, is unmarked.

Emuckfau Creek. *Photo courtesy of authors.*

Emuckfau Creek

Located just a few miles north of Horseshoe Bend, Emuckfau Creek is a small tributary of the Tallapoosa River. On January 22, 1814, Andrew Jackson's army was encamped near the creek on its way to the Red Stick village of Tohopeka at Horseshoe Bend when they were attacked by an army of Red Stick warriors. Jackson's men withstood the attack, but they soon learned that Tohopeka was too well fortified to assault and therefore retreated after the battle.

Emuckfau Creek is in present-day Tallapoosa County, and is within the borders of the Horseshoe Bend National Military Park. A marker commemorating the battle stands on Highway 22 near the community of New Site. Highway 49 crosses the creek just a few miles north of the military park.

Enitachopco Creek

As Andrew Jackson's army retreated back to Fort Strother after its encounter at Emuckfau Creek, the Red Sticks attacked it as it crossed Enitachopco Creek on January 24, 1814. Jackson's men withstood the attack and continued their retreat to Fort Strother.

Enitachopco Creek is northeast of Horseshoe Bend and meanders through Tallapoosa and Clay Counties. The exact location of the battlefield is unknown and there is no marker to commemorate the event. The creek can be accessed northwest of Goldville, Alabama, from a county road that runs off Highway 49.

Fort Armstrong

Located near the junction of the Coosa and Chattooga Rivers in northeast Alabama, Fort Armstrong was built by members of John Cocke's East Tennessee troops. The site may have been used by the British during the Revolutionary War. Some historians place Fort Lovell, an 1838 Cherokee removal post, at the site of Fort Armstrong.

Located in present-day Cherokee County, the fort site is under the waters of Weiss Lake near the town of Cedar Bluff. No historic marker exists.

Reconstruction of Fort Jackson. *Photo courtesy of authors.*

Andrew Jackson marker at the site of Fort Jackson. *Photo courtesy of authors.*

Fort Deposit

Fort Deposit served as one of Andrew Jackson's primary bases of supply during his campaign against the Red Sticks. Built in October 1813, the fort was located on the Tennessee River at the mouth of Thompson's Creek, three miles downriver from Gunter's Landing.

The site of the fort lies near the present-day town of Guntersville, Alabama, north of Guntersville Lake, near County Road 14. There is no historical marker designating the site.

Fort Jackson/Hickory Ground

After the American victory at Horseshoe Bend, Andrew Jackson led his men southward toward the Hickory Ground at the confluence of the Coosa and Tallapoosa Rivers, believed to be the last major gathering spot for Red Sticks. Finding no resistance, Jackson's troops helped construct Fort Jackson on the site where the French had built Fort Toulouse in 1717. Fort Jackson became a gathering place for surrendering Red Sticks and friendly Creeks in search of food. The epic meeting of Jackson and William Weatherford took place here, as well as the signing of the climatic

Fort Strother monument. *Photo courtesy of authors.*

Treaty of Fort Jackson in which the Creeks ceded twenty-three million acres to the United States.

Fort Toulouse–Fort Jackson Historic Site is located off U.S. 231 in Wetumpka, Alabama. The site contains a replica of the French fort and a partial reconstruction of Fort Jackson. The site also contains reproduction Creek houses, a visitor center and museum, as well as a nature trail.

Fort Strother

Fort Strother served as the primary advance supply base during Andrew Jackson's campaigns against the Red Sticks. Named after John Strother, Jackson's topographical engineer, the fort was built in November 1813 on the Coosa River at a spot known as Ten Islands. From this fort, Jackson moved to relieve the friendly Creeks besieged at Talladega and later on launched a foray that resulted in the battles of Emuckfau and Enitachopco Creeks. Fort Strother was also the location where Jackson was forced to deal with the near mutiny of his troops.

A historic marker and interpretive signage for Fort Strother are located in St. Clair County on Highway 144 near the Henry-Neely Dam on the Coosa River.

Fort Williams

Located approximately thirty miles south of Fort Strother on the Coosa River at a place known as Three Islands, Fort Williams was built in March

Soldiers' graves near the site of Fort Williams. *Photo courtesy of authors.*

1814. Named after the colonel of the Thirty-ninth U.S. Regiment, the fort served as the launching point for Jackson's march against the Red Sticks at Horseshoe Bend.

The site of Fort Williams is now under the Coosa River. A historic marker and cemetery containing the graves of Creek War veterans is near the site, east of Fayetteville, Alabama, on General Jackson Memorial Drive. The road is just off County Road 8 in a residential development on the Coosa River near Cedar Creek.

Hillabee Towns

The Hillabees were one of the most hostile groups of Red Stick Creeks. Although they had proposed peace to Andrew Jackson following the Red Stick defeat at the Battle of Talladega, another force of Tennessee militia unaware of their intention to surrender attacked and destroyed their towns in November 1813. Surviving Hillabee Creeks afterward pledged to fight to the death due to the perceived betrayal by Jackson, and many of them were on hand at Horseshoe Bend.

The location of the various Hillabee towns has not been documented, and there are no historical markers that commemorate their existence.

Overlook of the battlefield at Horseshoe Bend. *Photo courtesy of authors.*

Battle of Talladega monument. *Photo courtesy of authors.*

Horseshoe Bend/Tohopeka

Located in a sharp bend of the Tallapoosa River, Horseshoe Bend was the site of the decisive battle that effectively ended the Creek War. Red Sticks built the village of Tohopeka, containing over three hundred log huts, inside the bend in December 1813, and by the time of the battle, over 1,000 warriors and approximately 350 women and children had settled there. Jackson's force overwhelmed the Red Sticks on March 27, 1814, killing nearly 900 while suffering fewer than 200 casualties.

Horseshoe Bend National Military Park is the best interpreted site of the Creek War. Located in Tallapoosa County near Highway 49, the battlefield at Horseshoe Bend, administered by the National Park Service, consists of a visitor center containing a museum and a brief interpretive film. A self-guided tour takes you to various sites on the property where the battle unfolded.

Leroy Pope Mansion

Andrew Jackson allegedly visited this estate in Huntsville in 1814 on his trip northward after the Creek War had ended.

Near the mansion, now a private residence on Echols Street in downtown Huntsville, is a historic marker relating the mansion's history.

Talladega

Talladega was a friendly Creek village located thirty miles from Fort Strother. Upon learning that Talladega was under siege by Red Sticks, Jackson led his troops there and fought and won the Battle of Talladega on November 9, 1813.

A historic marker on the grounds of the county courthouse on the square in downtown Talladega explains the battle. Also in Talladega, a more elaborate monument that provides more detailed information on the battle stands just off Highway 21 south of the city. The friendly Creek village was supposedly located on the current site of a city cemetery a few blocks east of the battlefield monument. Another monument commemorating the battle lies inside the cemetery.

Tallushatchee

Tennessee forces, under the direct command of John Coffee, defeated a Red Stick contingent at Tallushatchee on November 3, 1813. The Red Stick village was located less than ten miles from Fort Strother on the Coosa River.

As of the printing of this book, the historic marker interpreting the battle placed on Highway 431 near Alexandria, Alabama, in Calhoun County is missing. The site of the battle is located just off Calhoun County Road 144, a mile west of U.S. 431. Not far from this location stands a marker memorializing Lyncoya, the Creek orphan from the battle whom Jackson adopted.

Securing the Gulf South

"By the eternal, they shall not sleep on our soil!…Gentlemen, the British are below; we must fight them tonight."
—*Major General Andrew Jackson*
before attacking the British, December 23, 1814

With the conclusion of the Creek War, the larger War of 1812 now took center stage in the Gulf South. Even though the United States had been at war with Great Britain since June 1812, open conflict between American and British forces in the region had been long in coming. For more than two years, the war had been fought in faraway places such as along the Canadian border, the northwestern frontier and the East Coast. Having finally defeated Napoleon in Europe, the British could now more strongly assert their military power; thus, they formulated a plan for bringing the war to a close. The plan called for British forces to sweep southward from Canada into New York, splicing the disaffected New England states from the rest of the Union. The plan also included a series of strategic raids against seaports and coastal cities in the Chesapeake Bay region and an attack on the weak American defenses along the Gulf Coast. Though the first two parts of the British plan had met with mixed results, the third, to be commanded by Rear Admiral Alexander Inglis Cochrane, showed signs of promise.

The British based their hopes in large part on the presence of Red Stick Creeks in the Gulf Coast region. Britain had long known that the Southern Indians could become potential allies against the United States. As early as the spring of 1814, Admiral Cochrane began planning ways to cultivate their friendship and provide them with arms in hopes of using them in an offensive along the Gulf Coast. In May of that year, Cochrane sent Captain Hugh Pigot to link up with the Creeks near present-day Apalachicola, Florida, located east of the headquarters of the local Spanish government in Pensacola.

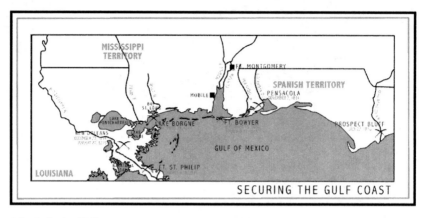

Map by Jessica McCarty.

Britain's war against the United States in the region, however, put Spanish officials in a delicate situation. For years, Spain's hold on the Florida peninsula had been slowly weakening. Spanish leaders had hoped to use the Creeks as a buffer against American encroachment and at times had provided the Red Sticks with supplies. Although the British landing on the Gulf Coast represented an affront to Spanish sovereignty, Spanish leaders secretly hoped that the British could help them defend the region from the ever-encroaching Americans. Reluctantly, they allowed the British to use Florida as a base from which to launch their campaign.

When Pigot landed in Florida on May 10, 1814, he was astonished to find hundreds of Red Stick refugees gathered there in desperate need of food. As Pigot began providing them with supplies, he learned the details of their defeat at Horseshoe Bend and realized that British cooperation had come too late. Had they arrived months earlier, Pigot could have better supplied the Red Sticks and either prolonged or even altered the outcome of the Creek War. Nevertheless, Pigot reported to his superiors that some three thousand Indians, most of them unarmed and starving, were available and still eager to fight the Americans. He established his camp farther up the Apalachicola River, at Prospect Bluff, and awaited further orders.

Convinced that he could rely on a strong force of Red Sticks to support his operation, Cochrane began detailing his plans for an offensive along the Gulf Coast. Informed that the Gulf South region had fewer than three thousand scattered American troops, he decided to strike first at Mobile, which would allow the British to then proceed northward up the Alabama River Valley and establish contact with additional Creek allies. From there, Cochrane's force would strike for Baton Rouge, thereby isolating New

Orleans. British leadership believed the capture of that important city would be relatively easy, as they thought residents of New Orleans resented American occupation and would not rally to defend the city.

Cochrane pressed forward with his plan, sending one hundred British marines under the command of Major Edward Nicolls to Prospect Bluff with orders to train and supply the Red Sticks. He also had the authority to equip and train the hundreds of escaped slaves who had recently fled to the British fort. Shortly after his August 10, 1814 arrival, Nicolls also learned that Creeks in Pensacola eagerly awaited the chance to fight the Americans, if they too could be fed. At the request of British agents in Pensacola and the city's Spanish officials, Nicolls moved his force west to help defend the city in the face of the belligerent posture of Andrew Jackson.

The ink had not yet dried on the Treaty of Fort Jackson when Old Hickory first focused his attention on what he thought were the real instigators of war—the British and the Spanish. As head of the U.S. Seventh Military District, Jackson knew of British plans for an offensive, as well as their intention to utilize Red Sticks in the effort. He had also heard that thousands of veteran British soldiers would soon arrive from Europe to assist in operations on the coast. Harboring a longtime hatred of the British, Jackson told his wife, "I owe to Britain a debt of retaliatory vengeance," and made plans to thwart the British campaign. He also wrote to the Spanish Governor Don Matteo Gonzalez Manrique in Pensacola, informing him that he knew about the renegade Creeks in his territory under the sway of the British and demanded that the Spanish solve this problem. In late August, Jackson moved his headquarters to Mobile, closer to the developing threat, and began strengthening Fort Bowyer, located on Mobile Point, in order to better guard Mobile Bay.

As Jackson improved the defenses of the entire Gulf Coast, the British moved forward with their plans to bring the region under their control. As the first steps toward that goal, Nicolls and his force of one hundred British soldiers, five hundred Native Americans and one hundred blacks seized control of Pensacola from the indecisive Spanish leadership. With this valuable base of operations secured for a British expedition, Cochrane next took aim at Fort Bowyer.

Containing twenty guns and 158 men under the command of Major William Lawrence, Fort Bowyer constituted the primary line of defense for Mobile Bay and the city itself. On September 12, 1814, 250 British soldiers and Native Americans landed near the fort to assault it from the rear, while a naval squadron of four ships moved into position to bombard

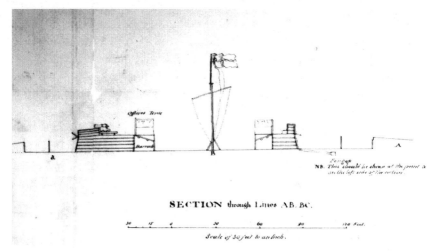

SECTION through Lines AB BC.

Sketch of Fort Bowyer, by Colonel Alexander Dickson. *Courtesy of Fort Morgan State Historic Site.*

it from Mobile Bay. Despite British superiority in numbers and firepower, the American defenders repelled both the British land and naval forces. While British losses numbered almost eighty, American forces suffered only four killed and five wounded. Even more costly for the British, during the September 15 naval attack, the Americans severely damaged the British frigate *Hermes* so badly that it was eventually destroyed. The British had no choice but to limp back to Pensacola and rethink their plan of attack.

Angered at Spanish complicity in the British offensive, Jackson planned an attack against Pensacola to destroy the British forces stationed there. As an added benefit, he hoped to crush the remaining Red Sticks who had fled to Pensacola after Horseshoe Bend. He requested permission from authorities in Washington to move on Pensacola, but was admonished not to invade the territory and disrupt Spain's neutrality. Weary of what he viewed as senseless delay, Jackson decided to take action himself. Gathering a force of four thousand men consisting of regulars, militia and Native American allies at Fort Montgomery, he moved on Pensacola in early November. Admitting in a letter to Secretary of State James Monroe that he acted without orders, he explained his reasons for invading Spanish Florida with confidence that the administration would eventually justify his actions.

Jackson arrived outside Pensacola on November 6, 1814. He immediately sent word to the Spanish governor that, although he came not as an enemy of Spain, he demanded that British forces evacuate

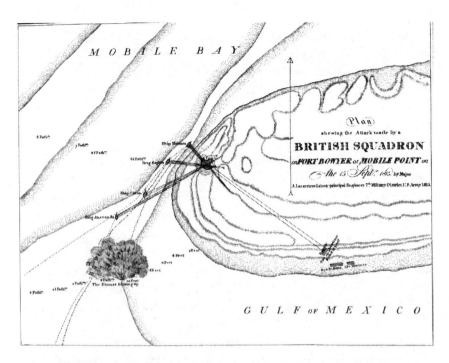

"Plan showing the Attack made by a British squadron on Fort Bowyer at Mobile Point on the 15th September 1814," by Arsène LaCarrière Latour. *Courtesy of the Historic New Orleans Collection.*

"Hermes vs. Bowyer," by Sidney Schell. *Courtesy of Fort Morgan State Historic Site.*

the forts of the town. Despite the deplorable behavior of the British in Pensacola, the Spanish recognized that because of the feebleness of their garrison, their only hope of defense of the region lay in an alliance with the British. The governor therefore denied Jackson's demands.

Jackson wasted no time, attacking on November 7. Leaving a small force on the west side of the town as a feint, he moved the majority of his men to the east side of the town and attacked. The plan worked to perfection on the surprised defenders, and the operation ended within a matter of minutes. Governor Manrique himself sought out the Americans to surrender. Yet the limited resistance provided the British enough time to destroy Fort Barrancas, the key fort protecting Pensacola Bay, and to retreat from the area. At a cost of fewer than twenty casualties, Jackson had delivered a severe blow to British plans on the Gulf Coast. His mission accomplished, and with Pensacola no longer defensible due to the loss of Fort Barrancas, Jackson returned the town to Spanish authorities.

Having learned of British intentions to attack New Orleans, Jackson next moved to counter that threat. First, he returned to Mobile to strengthen its defenses. Not completely convinced that New Orleans would be the main British objective, Jackson initially concluded that it made more sense for them to capture Mobile first and use it as a base for further operations. Jackson finally accepted that New Orleans had indeed become the main British target only after receiving additional

"Blowing up of Fort Barrancas in 1814." *Courtesy of State Archives of Florida.*

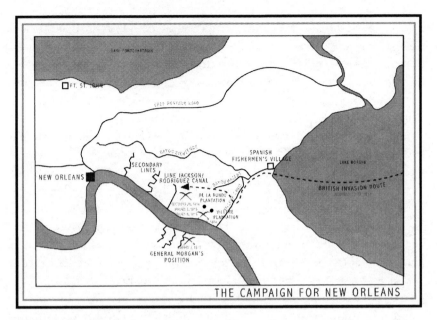

THE CAMPAIGN FOR NEW ORLEANS

Map by Jessica McCarty.

intelligence. Leaving James Winchester in charge of Mobile's defenses, he left on November 22, arriving in the Crescent City on December 1.

Upon arriving, Jackson urged the citizens—a heterogeneous population of French, Spanish, Creoles, free blacks, slaves and Americans—to put their differences aside and unite to defend the city against the British invaders. He organized the forces at his disposal, which included local militia, a company of free blacks, some friendly Choctaws, two U.S. Infantry regiments and cavalry under his trusted subordinate, John Coffee. He also eagerly awaited the arrival of additional Tennessee and Kentucky militia that he had earlier requested. Despite first refusing the services of "pirate" Jean Laffite, he reluctantly accepted his aid and that of his "hellish banditi," in large part because of the arms and ammunition that they could provide. Laffite, as leader of the group based near Barataria Bay on the Louisiana coast, had earlier entertained overtures from the British before ultimately deciding to side with the Americans. His support would prove critical to Jackson during the coming battle.

Regardless of the composition of his force, Jackson's defense of New Orleans faced difficulties because several possible routes of approach existed for the British, all of which the Americans could not defend simultaneously. Since the British navy could invest the city only via the

Mississippi River, Jackson ordered improvements to Fort St. Philip below New Orleans. Concerned about a possible approach through Lake Borgne, Jackson had eastern routes to the city scouted and defended. He relied heavily on his small naval force of five gunboats in the gulf, commanded by Thomas ap Catesby Jones, to watch for the approaching British navy and to provide a defensive cover for the lake.

Jones and his flotilla did not have to wait long. Having failed at Mobile and Pensacola, Admiral Cochrane had determined to target New Orleans directly. He gathered an invasion force in Jamaica, which included British forces returning from their forays along the Chesapeake, as well as troops fresh off their European victory over Napoleon. The fleet left Jamaica on November 26, 1814, and by December 8, it had gathered off the Chandeleur Islands, when it was spotted by the American fleet. Although Jones wanted to retreat to a better position under the guns of Fort Petites Coquilles, an adverse eastern wind forced the American boats to make a stand. The British unloaded more than 1,200 men into forty-five barges equipped with forty-three guns and moved forward. Known as the Battle of Lake Borgne, the December 14 action lasted only forty-five minutes. Although the American boats contained only 183 men and twenty-three guns, they fought bravely and destroyed a few British boats before being overwhelmed. The defeat represented a huge loss for Jackson—he could

"Battle of Lake Borgne," by Thomas L. Hornbrook. *Courtesy of the Historic New Orleans Collection (1950.54).*

no longer monitor British operations, could not communicate with Mobile and, more importantly, had lost control of the lake to the British.

Exploiting their advantage would require tremendous effort on the part of the British. With the help of spies who had conducted reconnaissance of the routes to New Orleans, Cochrane chose to land near Bayou Bienvenue. To get there, British soldiers had to be ferried nearly forty miles in shallow draft boats to Pea Island, near the mouth of the Pearl River. Sailors struggled as they transported the soldiers to the island, where the troops endured a miserable encampment because of cold and wet conditions. From there, sailors rowed them some thirty miles through Lake Borgne to a fishermen's village on Bayou Bienvenue. This arduous process began on December 17, and by December 23, the lead elements of the British army had arrived at Bayou Bienvenue. Led by General John Keane, who at this point commanded the British land force, the British moved ashore unopposed. They followed along Bienvenue until they reached Bayou Mazant, where they eventually disembarked to continue their invasion. By 11:00 a.m., the British advance guard arrived at General Jacques Villeré's house, where they surrounded the American scouts posted to guard against

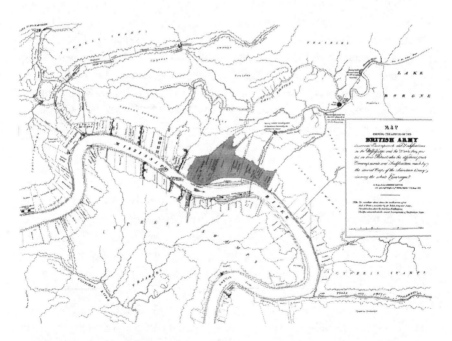

"A map showing the Landing of the British Army, its several encampments and fortifications on the Mississippi and the works they erected on their retreat," by Arsène LaCarrière Latour. *Courtesy of the Historic New Orleans Collection.*

Villerè's House. *From Benson J. Lossing,* The Pictorial Field-Book of the War of 1812.

their approach. Villeré's son, Gabriel, narrowly escaped, fleeing to New Orleans to warn Jackson that the British had arrived.

When Jackson received word of the danger, he sent his chief engineer Major Arsène Lacarrière Latour to ascertain the situation. Latour confirmed that the British had arrived with nearly sixteen hundred troops, prompting Jackson to exclaim, "By the eternal, they shall not sleep on our soil!" Jackson hastily gathered an approximately equal force to make a strike at the invaders. Fortunately for the American army, Keane halted his forces, in large part because he had heard rumors that Jackson had as many as twenty thousand men. Had Keane pushed forward immediately, New Orleans might well have fallen that very day.

Jackson's attack was a combined army-navy operation. He divided his force into two wings. On the right near the river he placed his regulars, Louisiana volunteers, men from New Orleans, free blacks and Choctaws. On the left, he placed Coffee and the Mississippi Dragoons under Thomas Hinds. To support his attack, he ordered Naval Commander Daniel Patterson to send the fourteen-gun *Carolina* down the river to bombard the British. The boat's opening salvo, fired at 7:30 p.m. on December 23, signaled Jackson's force to move forward.

Although completely caught off guard and initially pushed back, the British eventually slowed the American advance. Characterized by confusion, the battle featured close, hand-to-hand combat made all the more chaotic because of the darkness and fog. After about two hours,

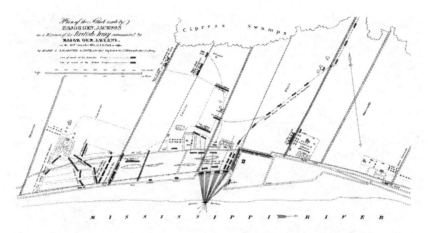

"Plan of the Attack made by Major Gen. Andrew Jackson on a Division of the British Army commanded by Major Gen. J. Keane on the 23d December, 1814, at 7 o'clock at night," by Arsène LaCarrière Latour. *Courtesy of the Historic New Orleans Collection.*

Jackson disengaged and pulled his men back, eventually setting up a defense around an old millrace known as the Rodriguez Canal. Both sides had suffered more than two hundred casualties. Technically a draw, this opening engagement brought the British advance on New Orleans to an immediate halt. Almost as importantly, it dispelled British notions that they would easily push the ragtag American army aside and capture the "Beauty and Booty" that supposedly awaited them in New Orleans.

At the same time in Europe, diplomats had already drafted the treaty that would end the war. On December 24, British and American representatives signed the Treaty of Ghent. Although the treaty ended hostilities, it did not solve any of the issues that had started the war. Instead, it simply returned conditions to as they had been before the conflict.

Back along the Mississippi, Jackson began strengthening his position on the Rodriguez Canal, a four-feet-wide and ten-feet-deep rampart that stretched nearly three quarters of a mile from the river into a swamp. Jackson had immediately put his men to work piling mud to make the rampart higher and digging to make the ditch deeper and wider. He also had them place batteries, eventually eight in all, along the line. Soon, Jackson's men had created a formidable defensive position that would be difficult to overwhelm.

On Christmas Day 1814, Sir Edward Michael Pakenham finally arrived to take command of the British expedition. The brother-in-law of the Duke of Wellington, Pakenham had gained distinction fighting the

"Peace of Ghent 1814 and triumph of America," by Mme. Plantou. *Courtesy of the Library of Congress.*

French on the Spanish Peninsula and looked forward to future glories in Louisiana. His outlook changed drastically once he viewed the situation in which his army sat. Though he recognized the dreadful position in which he had been placed and chastised the army leadership for not moving to take the city as soon as they landed, he determined to press on.

Pakenham immediately took the offensive. He had his artillery fire hot shot at the U.S. gunboat *Carolina* and the newly arrived *Louisiana*, which had been raking the British lines on a continual basis. Much to the improvement of British morale, this bombardment set the *Carolina* on fire and forced the *Louisiana* to pull back. On December 28, Pakenham tested the American line with a two-pronged foray. Near the river, he sent a column under the command of John Keane forward, but American fire from soldiers along the canal, as well as by the *Louisiana* now stationed alongside the American fortification, halted the attack. On the British right, nearer the swamps, a force under Samuel Gibbs had better success. Gibbs nearly breached the American lines before Pakenham, who had witnessed the failure of his troops closer to the river, pulled him back. The British suffered approximately fifty casualties in this "reconnaissance-in-force," while the Americans had fewer than twenty.

Undeterred, Pakenham decided to attempt to weaken the American lines with an artillery bombardment. To achieve maximum results, he requested additional guns be brought from the British ships. During the next three days, sailors and soldiers in a Herculean effort transported fourteen large guns from the British fleet into position. All together, Pakenham had six batteries containing thirty guns prepared to blast the American position to oblivion.

At approximately ten o'clock on New Year's Day 1815, the British guns opened fire. The barrage surprised the American army, which had gathered for a grand review. Over the next few hours, both sides lobbed hundreds of shells at one another. Whereas many of the British shells harmlessly embedded themselves into the mud of Jackson's line, the American return fire wreaked havoc on the poorly constructed British batteries. By the time the bombardment had ended, all six batteries had suffered damage and the British had lost several guns. When the smoke cleared, Jackson had suffered fewer than forty casualties, and his line at the Rodriguez Canal held firm. The American barrage killed and wounded nearly one hundred British soldiers. Perhaps even worse, British morale plummeted. The British high command had no choice but to wait for additional reinforcements and formulate a new plan to break Jackson's line.

Jackson used the idle time wisely, shoring up his position with the assistance of his chief engineer, Major Latour. His entrenched position, referred to as "Line Jackson," was further strengthened by the addition of an advance redoubt that was built on his right, near the river. Manning his line, from the river toward the swamps, were regulars from the Seventh U.S. Regiment, New Orleans riflemen, Louisiana volunteers, free men of color, the Forty-fourth U.S. Regiment, William Carroll's Tennesseans, and finally, on the extreme left guarding the swamp, Coffee's men and several dozen Choctaw braves. Recently arrived Kentuckians, most of them unarmed, and cavalry from Louisiana and Mississippi formed the reserves. Eight batteries manned by regulars, along with many of Laffite's Baratarians, who provided much-needed ammunition and powder, also held the line.

Jackson's focus on the Rodriguez Canal came at the neglect of the far weaker defenses on the west bank of the river. Not long after the battle on December 23, Jackson had sent men to the west bank to create another line. A few hundred Louisianans under General David Morgan manned this position, supported by some of the poorly supplied and outfitted Kentuckians. Morgan's failure to set up his position where Latour had suggested exasperated the problem. This weak position, manned by inadequate troops and an ineffective leader, proved an inviting target for the British.

Hoping to seize this opportunity, Pakenham planned to send fourteen hundred men under Colonel William Thornton across the river to capture the west bank position. At the same time, he planned an assault on Line Jackson. The main attack would be led by Major General Samuel Gibbs, who would attack near Jackson's weakest position along the swamp. Men under John Keane would storm the advanced redoubt by the river. A third brigade, under recently arrived General John Lambert, would act as reserve.

Logistical difficulties ruined Pakenham's carefully laid plans. Soldiers and sailors spent several backbreaking days widening and deepening Villeré's canal to be able to bring boats in to transport troops across the river for the attack on the west bank. This task became even more difficult because of numerous cave-ins on the improved canal. With the main attack on Line Jackson scheduled for the early morning hours of January 8, Thornton could not wait for all the boats to arrive and had to begin crossing his troops immediately. During the night of the seventh and the early morning hours of the eighth, his men crossed, but the river's current pushed them downstream farther than anticipated, causing additional delay in the British attack.

Pakenham learned that Thornton's men had gotten off late, but he decided to launch the main assault anyway. Beginning their assault with the launch of a signal rocket, the British columns surged forward in a fog soon blown aside by the wind. Jackson and his men greeted the attack with artillery and musketry fire. Chaos and delay continued to ruin British chances for success. Pakenham chose the Forty-fourth Regiment to lead the assault on Jackson's left near the swamps, but the regiment did not have the necessary fascines and ladders to scale the American position and were in the rear gathering the equipment when the assault began. Gibbs led other troops forward, but many of them stopped to return fire instead of pressing toward the American line, which led to heavy casualties under the murderous fire from the Americans. General Keane personally led the Ninety-third Highlanders, one of the army's elite units, diagonally across the field to reinforce the attack on the right, but they too absorbed heavy casualties. On the British left, close to the river, the attack achieved some success. Using the fog as cover, troops led by Colonel

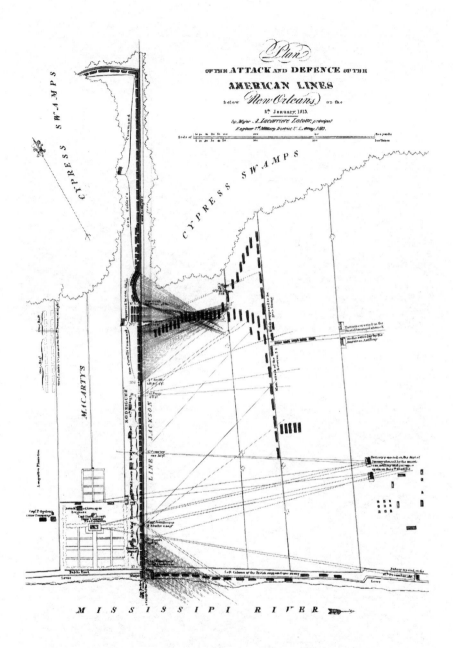

"Plan of the Attack and Defense of the American lines below New Orleans, on the 8th January, 1815," by Arsène LaCarrière Latour. *Courtesy of the Historic New Orleans Collection.*

"Battle of New Orleans," by Jean Hyacinthe de Laclotte. *Courtesy of the Historic New Orleans Collection (1971.53).*

"A Correct view of the battle near the city of New Orleans," by Francisco Scachi. *Courtesy of the Library of Congress.*

Robert Rennie captured the advanced American redoubt, but soon, the fire from the main American line proved too much for the British, forcing them to pull back.

The Americans kept up a steady, murderous fire on the British during the assault. Artillery and rifle fire tore holes in British lines as they moved across the open field. British infantrymen and their officer corps fell by the hundreds. Pakenham himself suffered several wounds before dying. Gibbs and Rennie also died on the battlefield and Keane was seriously wounded. General Lambert, assuming command of the army, prepared to send his reserves forward before concluding the day was lost.

The British assault on Line Jackson failed miserably, but events on the west bank proved as disastrous to the Americans. Lambert had called off the main attack by the time Thornton and his force began their work against Morgan's weak defenses. Thornton quickly pushed aside an advance guard and then overwhelmed General Morgan's main position. Morgan's poorly armed and trained men got off a volley or two and then scrambled away. Thornton sought to follow up his victory when he received word from Lambert to pull back and recross the river. Had Thornton's assault been on time and had he taken the American battery

"The American Riflemen, After the Battle, Rescuing the Wounded British," *Courtesy of the Historic New Orleans Collection (1974.25.5.7).*

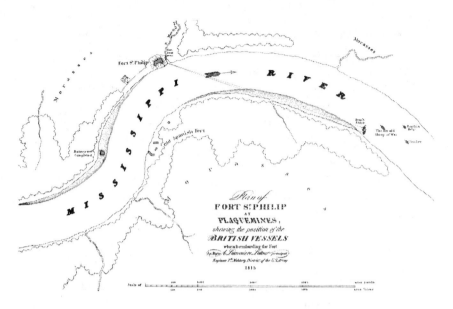

"Plan of Fort St. Philip at Plaquemines, showing the position of the British vessels when Bombarding the Fort," by Arsène LaCarrière Latour. *Courtesy of the Historic New Orleans Collection.*

established by Patterson prior to the main attack, the outcome of the main assault at Line Jackson might have been different.

Casualty figures reveal what a decisive victory Jackson's army had won. In less than two hours, the British suffered more than 2,000 casualties: 291 killed, 1,262 wounded and 484 captured. American losses were slight in comparison, with 13 killed, 39 wounded and only 19 missing. Highlighting the severity of the British defeat, the battlefield in front of Jackson's line lay literally covered with dead and wounded British soldiers.

Though severely shaken, the British undertook one last attempt to capture the city. Admiral Cochrane moved his fleet upriver from the Gulf of Mexico. Beginning on January 9, the British fleet began a bombardment of Fort St. Philip, the only true obstacle preventing the British from taking the city from this route. Yet ten days of constant shelling failed to reduce the fort. Unable to advance, the British fleet retreated amid the cheers of the Americans. By this time, Lambert had already removed his army from the field. His men improved the route back to Lake Borgne after their assault on January 8 and began their retreat from the area after midnight on January 18. On January 27, 1815, the British fleet left the area for good.

Although Jackson and his troops took part in various celebrations and reviews during the next few days, Old Hickory remained vigilant. He maintained martial law in New Orleans and waited for the next move by the British.

After departing the Mississippi, Admiral Cochrane decided to revert back to the original British plan and attempt to capture Mobile again. This time, he allocated more resources to capture Fort Bowyer. More than six hundred troops with artillery went ashore to attack the fort by land, while British ships prepared for a simultaneous bombardment. American commander William Lawrence understood his position to be hopeless, and on February 11, he surrendered the fort and its nearly four hundred men. British preparations for capturing Mobile were well underway when word of the Treaty of Ghent finally arrived, thereby ending military operations.

With the war now seemingly over, only the British fort at Prospect Bluff remained a threat to the United States. After Jackson had captured Pensacola in November, Major Nicolls and his Native American and black allies retreated back to their camp at Prospect Bluff. Their numbers continued to grow as more Native American refugees joined them. Nicolls eventually learned that the war had ended, but one section of the Treaty of Ghent complicated matters. In Article IX of the treaty, the United States agreed that all Indian tribes still at war with the United States could have all their rights and land restored to them. According to the British, this nullified the previous Treaty of Fort Jackson and the Creek cession of twenty-three million acres of land. The United States government interpreted things differently, insisting that it had already made peace with the Creeks by the time of the Treaty of Ghent. Nicolls continued to hold his position at Prospect Bluff, waiting for the Americans to uphold Article IX of the Treaty of Ghent and restore Creek lands. He even travelled to England with Red Stick leader Josiah Francis to plead his case. In the end, England chose not to press the issue, abandoning the Creeks to their fate.

British forces finally withdrew from the area in June 1815 along with most of those Native Americans who had resided there. Only the former slaves remained. In time, the position at Prospect Bluff came to be known as the "Negro Fort," as more than five hundred blacks remained. The fort's existence became quite an embarrassment to the United States, as well as to Spanish officials in Florida, with whom the United States pleaded to handle the problem. Eventually, U.S. troops reduced the fort in July 1816. During a brief engagement, an artillery shell struck a powder magazine inside the fort, destroying it and killing almost everyone inside. The fort's destruction ended the Creek War and the War of 1812 in the Gulf South.

Site of the American line along the Rodriguez Canal during the Battle of New Orleans. The Chalmette Monument is at right. *Photo courtesy of authors.*

Historic Sites

British Invasion Route

Many of the sites associated with the British invasion route, such as Cat Island, Pea Island and the Fisherman's Village, are only accessible by boat. Bayou Bienvenue, the route followed by the British to Chalmette, is crossed by Louisiana Highway 47 south of Highway 90.

Chalmette

The Battle of New Orleans took place on the grounds of the Chalmette and McCarty plantations along the Mississippi River below the city. The central defensive feature of the battlefield was "Line Jackson," located along the Rodriguez Canal separating the plantations. From this position, constructed over a two-week period by the Americans, Jackson's men withstood an artillery bombardment and one minor attack prior to the main British assault on January 8, 1815. The attack failed to crack the American defenses and cost the British over two thousand casualties. Jackson's victory here was the greatest of the war and ranks as one of the most decisive victories in American military history.

Chalmette National Battlefield, a division of Jean Laffite National Historical Park, is located on St. Bernard Highway (Louisiana Highway 46), six miles from New Orleans. The park features a driving tour of the battlefield and a partial reconstruction of the Rodriguez Canal Line. Chalmette National Cemetery, containing the graves of four Americans who fought in the War of 1812, adjoins the site. A new visitor's center, replacing the one that was destroyed in 2005 by Hurricane Katrina, was dedicated in January 2011.

De La Ronde House

The plantation home of Pierre Denis de la Ronde was used as a British hospital during the Battle of New Orleans.

The ruins of the house are located on St. Bernard Highway (Louisiana Highway 46), a short distance east of Chalmette Battlefield. Across the street is a monument identifying the spot where Louisiana militia camped on December 23, 1814.

Fort Barrancas today. *Photo courtesy of authors.*

Fort Barrancas (Fort San Carlos de Barrancas)

Built by the Spanish around 1797 on the site of a former British redoubt, Fort Barrancas guarded the entrance to Pensacola Bay. When General Andrew Jackson captured Pensacola in November 1814, British soldiers blew up the fort as they evacuated the area.

Fort Barrancas, reconstructed by American engineers in 1844, is now a historic site administered by the National Park Service as part of the Gulf Islands National Seashore. The fort is located on Highway 295 (Navy Boulevard), which runs through the Pensacola Naval Air Station.

Fort Bowyer

Named after colonel John Bowyer, Fort Bowyer was a wooden fortification built at the end of Mobile Point to guard the entrance to Mobile Bay. The British attacked the fort on two occasions during the War of 1812. Major William Lawrence, in command of a group of regular soldiers, repulsed the first attack in September 1814. The second assault, launched after the battle of New Orleans in February 1815, resulted in Lawrence's surrender of the fort.

Fort Bowyer was later replaced by Fort Morgan, made famous for its role in the defense of Mobile Bay during the Civil War. Fort Morgan Historic Site lies at the end of Highway 180, twenty-two miles west of

Mobile Point monument at Fort Morgan State Historic Site. *Photo courtesy of authors.*

Highway 59 in Gulf Shores, Alabama. Visitors may take a self-guided tour of the fort and view a small museum, which contains a small exhibit interpreting Fort Bowyer's role in the War of 1812.

Fort Montgomery

Fort Montgomery, named for Major Lemuel Montgomery, was built in 1814 a few miles from the site of Fort Mims by Colonel Thomas Benton to serve as a supply base. General Andrew Jackson gathered a force at the fort before moving on to Pensacola in November 1814. Later, the fort was occupied by troops under Major Uriah Blue while conducting raids against Red Sticks.

The site of Fort Montgomery is believed to be just west of Highway 59 in Baldwin County, Alabama, about two miles southeast of Fort Mims. The site is unmarked, and its exact location is unknown.

Fort Petites Coquilles

Fort Petites Coquilles was a small, unfinished fort that guarded the pass through the Rigolets into Lake Pontchartrain at the time of the War of 1812. American Lieutenant Thomas ap Catesby Jones attempted to pull his boats under the protection of the fort before the Battle of Lake Borgne, but the winds failed him, leaving his small fleet trapped and forced to give battle unprotected. Overestimating the fort's strength, the British decided not to test the fort's defenses and sought another route to New Orleans.

In 1818, Fort Pike was built at the site of Fort Petites Coquilles to better defend the Rigolets. Fort Pike Historic Site is located in Orleans Parish on Highway 90 north of New Orleans.

Fort St. Philip

Often referred to as the "key to Louisiana," Fort St. Philip was located eighty miles south of New Orleans and protected the city from an assault up the river from its mouth. During the campaign for New Orleans, the fort contained over thirty guns and a garrison of approximately four hundred. From January 9 to 18, 1815, Fort St. Philip withstood a nine-day bombardment from the British navy following Jackson's victory at New Orleans.

Fort St. Philip is located in Plaquemines Parish, thirty miles north of the mouth of the Mississippi River. Situated on the east bank, the fort site lies on private property and is only accessible by boat. Located almost directly across the river from the site is Fort Jackson, a fort constructed in the 1830s. The site, located off Louisiana Highway 23 near Venice, was severely damaged by Hurricane Katrina and has only recently reopened.

Lake Borgne

Lake Borgne was the site of the largest naval battle on the Gulf Coast during the War of 1812. On December 14, 1814, a fleet of forty-five British barges under Captain Thomas Lockyer defeated five American gunboats led by Lieutenant Thomas ap Catesby Jones guarding the lake near Malheureux Island. The battle gave the British control over the lake and many avenues of invasion into New Orleans.

The site of the Battle of Lake Borgne is only accessible by boat. A historical marker commemorating the conflict once stood on Beach Boulevard in Bay St. Louis, Mississippi, but was destroyed during Hurricane Katrina.

New Orleans

New Orleans was a highly sought prize by the British army. By the time of the War of 1812, the city, founded by the French in 1718, had become the Gulf Coast's chief port, as well as one of the largest cities in the United States. Due to its diverse population, the British high command hoped its inhabitants would fail to support the American cause. Instead, Andrew Jackson rallied the citizens to form an army that fiercely defended the city. The British attempts to capture the city culminated in defeat at the Battle of New Orleans on January 8, 1815.

Jackson Square in New Orleans. *Photo courtesy of authors.*

Though still recovering from Hurricane Katrina, New Orleans remains a city proud of its culture and heritage. The heart of the city remains Jackson Square, formerly the Place d'Armes, where grand reviews of troops marched before and after the Battle of New Orleans. At the center of the square stands a magnificent statue of Andrew Jackson. The Cabildo, the central facility of the Louisiana State Museum complex and site of the signing of the Louisiana Purchase, contains exhibits on Louisiana history, including information on the War of 1812 and the Battle of New Orleans. The Historic New Orleans Collection also contains exhibits on the city's history, and its William C. Cook War of 1812 in the South Collection is a gem for researchers seeking primary source material on the conflict.

Pensacola

A key trading and population center of Spanish West Florida, Pensacola played an important role in the Creek War and the War of 1812. Red Sticks obtained supplies from the city throughout the conflict, first from Spanish authorities and British merchants and later from the British military. Determined to end these activities, Andrew Jackson captured Pensacola in November 1814. The city was protected by several fortifications, including Fort San Carlos de Barrancas, Fort San Miguel and Fort Santa Rosa.

Several sites associated with the Creek War and the War of 1812 can be found in downtown Pensacola today. The Colonial Archaeological Trail highlights several areas of Fort San Miguel, the principal Spanish fort that defended the town during the war. The T.T. Wentworth Jr. Florida State Museum and Pensacola Historical Society Museum contain exhibits concerning the time period. A statue of Andrew Jackson stands in Plaza Ferdinand, a park in the heart of downtown. A scale model of the headquarters of Panton, Leslie and Company, the British firm that dominated trade activities with Native Americans, stands on the site of the original business at the corner of Main and Baylen Streets.

Prospect Bluff

Prospect Bluff, a gathering spot for Native Americans located near a British-run trading house, was the site at which British agents supplied allied Red Sticks and black fugitives for their operations along the Gulf Coast. The British eventually built a fort on the site, which—following their evacuation from the area—was later occupied only by hundreds of black refugees and became known as the "Negro Fort." The outpost

Andrew Jackson monument in Plaza Ferdinand VII, downtown Pensacola, Florida. *Photo courtesy of authors.*

Site of Fort Gadsden at Prospect Bluff. *Photo courtesy of authors.*

proved to be an embarrassment for Spanish and American authorities. U.S. forces destroyed the fort in July 1816.

The site of the "Negro Fort," now known as Fort Gadsden Historic Site in honor of a later fort built on the site, is located in Franklin County, Florida, along the Apalachicola River just off of Highway 65. The site features a walking tour and exhibits that detail the history of the area.

West Bank

To prevent Jackson's mainline at the Rodriguez Canal from being hit with enfilade fire, American forces organized a defensive position on the opposite side of the Mississippi River. A contingent of British troops crossed the river on the morning of January 8, 1815, and assaulted this west bank position. American General David Morgan's poorly trained and equipped troops were defeated handily, but owing to poor timing, the British were unable to take advantage of the situation and were recalled shortly afterward to the eastern bank.

Little interpretation of the Battle of New Orleans exists on the western bank of the Mississippi River. A historical marker, which the authors have been unable to locate, allegedly stands in Aurora Gardens.

Conclusion

The Creek War and the War of 1812 had a tremendous impact on the history of the Gulf South and the United States as a whole. The war resulted in significant territorial expansion, secured large portions of the Southeast against European colonial powers, set a precedent for removal of Native Americans from their traditional homelands and led to the rise of one of the most influential military and political leaders in American history.

The most direct impact of the war on the country was the acquisition of territory. The Treaty of Fort Jackson provided the United States government with over twenty-three million acres of land, mostly in Georgia and the future state of Alabama, which would be rapidly settled by land-hungry white Americans and their slaves. In this "Great Migration," thousands of people poured into the Mississippi Territory in record numbers. The portion that became the state of Mississippi nearly doubled in population between 1810 and 1820, and the portion that became the state of Alabama grew even more rapidly. In 1810, 9,000 whites and blacks lived in this area; ten years later, nearly 150,000 people called the new state of Alabama home. Introduced to the fertile lands of the Old Southwest, these settlers developed an increased reliance on cotton agriculture, which was only accentuated after the widespread use of the cotton gin made the crop more profitable than ever. Ultimately, this development, underpinned by the institution of slavery, led the states of the Gulf South on the road toward secession and civil war.

More immediately, however, the forced removal of thousands of Creeks who lived in the lands affected by the treaty eliminated the buffer zone on which the Spanish had so heavily depended for the defense of Florida. Within half a decade, Florida would officially become a part of the United States. In addition, General James Wilkinson's capture of Mobile in 1812 and Andrew Jackson's victory at New Orleans forever solidified America's long-disputed claim to millions of acres of land in the

"Andrew Jackson with the Tennessee forces on the Hickory Grounds," by Breuker and Kessler. *Courtesy of the Library of Congress.*

region. Equally important, the Treaty of Fort Jackson set a precedent for the removal of Native Americans from the Southeast. Within thirty years after that landmark compact, the Choctaws, Chickasaws and Cherokees would follow the same path as the Creeks, as their land was taken from them and they were forced westward across the Mississippi River.

Andrew Jackson's rise to national prominence, however, ranks as the most significant outcome of the conflict. His indomitable will and military prowess made him the country's foremost military hero and allowed him to ride a wave of popularity all the way to the presidency. In two terms as the nation's chief executive, he exerted incredible influence on the development of the young nation. It is revealing that the time period of his greatest power is known today among historians as the "Jacksonian Era."

Jackson's reputation, however, has unfortunately suffered recently at the hands of historians and others who have harshly judged his handling of Native Americans and ignored his larger accomplishments. Jackson's concerns over national security initially led him to favor removal of Native Americans from the Gulf South in order to separate them from the ever-present influence of European powers who sought to use them as pawns against the United States. Jackson also sincerely believed that because of deep-seated cultural differences, Native Americans and white Americans would not be able to coexist peacefully in the region. The only way for native groups to survive, he thought, would be to move westward. While these notions seem preposterous today, we must remember that Jackson was a man of his time and must be judged as such. Even if some of his actions seem misguided over a century and a half after his death, his military and political talents, commitment to achieving goals in the face of extreme difficulty and amazing patriotism should still allow him a place in the pantheon of American heroes.

Perhaps most important to the development of the United States, Jackson and the War of 1812 provided the country with a powerful sense of nationalism that would propel its rise to global prominence. Holding its own against the world's greatest military power increased the nation's pride in itself and simultaneously legitimized the United States as a major player on the world stage. Jackson's improbable victory at New Orleans, utilizing a diverse force symbolic of the nation's immigrant heritage, served in its day as an inspirational reminder of just how far the country had come in only a few decades of independence. Today, as we approach the 200th anniversary of that victory at New Orleans, the triumph still resonates as one of the most dramatic turning points in our nation's history. Both it, and the larger struggle of which it was a part, are seminal events in our heritage that ought not be forgotten.

Biographies

David Adams

An officer in the Georgia militia, Major General David Adams led a raid on Creek towns on the upper Tallapoosa River in December 1813. His campaign resulted in the destruction of the town of Nuyaka.

John Armstrong

John Armstrong served as the U.S. secretary of war from January 1813 to September 1814. He called for the formation of the armies that would eventually crush Red Stick resistance and was one of the architects of the three-pronged strategy of attack they followed. Armstrong frequently clashed with his subordinates, often disregarded established chain-of-command procedures and was ultimately forced to resign in the wake of charges that he neglected the defenses of Washington, D.C., after that city fell to the British in the summer of 1814.

Jeremiah Austill

Jeremiah Austill became celebrated for his role in two daring episodes during the Creek War. Following the attack on Fort Sinquefield in September 1813, he rode alone forty miles at night to relate the news to General Claiborne at Mount Vernon, and returned the next day with orders for the settlers from the general. His most well-known exploit occurred a few months later, when he participated in the famous Canoe Fight.

Timpoochee Barnard

The son of a Scotch trader and a Yuchi woman, Timpoochee Barnard led a group of Yuchi warriors in support of U.S. forces during the war.

Jeremiah Austill in his later years. *From H.S. Halbert and T.H. Ball,* The Creek War of 1813 and 1814.

At the Battle of Calabee Creek, Barnard's command played a vital role in helping prevent the rout of General John Floyd's troops. Barnard later fought against Red Stick forces under General Andrew Jackson in the First Seminole War.

(Barnard's grave site is located in Fort Mitchell Historic Landmark Park on Highway 431 a few miles south of Phenix City, Alabama.)

Timpoochee Barnard. *Courtesy of the Columbus Museum (Gift of Henry Schwob, 1989.8).*

Daniel Beasley

Daniel Beasley, the commander of the garrison at Fort Mims, is most remembered for disregarding reports of Red Stick activity prior to their attack in August 1813. Largely as a result of his negligence, Red Sticks took the fort by total surprise. Beasley became one of the first casualties of the battle, as he was killed while trying to close one of the fort's open gates during the initial Red Stick charge.

Big Warrior (Tustunnuggee Thlucco)

Big Warrior, allegedly one of the largest of the Creeks in stature, was a prominent leader of allied Creeks who resided in the village of Tuckaubatchee. Though he welcomed Tecumseh to the town in 1811, he remained an ally of the United States once the conflict began. Red Sticks eventually forced him to leave Tuckaubatchee for his decision, and he relocated to Coweta, where in October 1813, he helped lead an attack on a band of Red Sticks. Big Warrior was among the first of the Creek dignitaries at the signing of the Treaty of Fort Jackson to speak against the agreement.

Willie Blount

Willie Blount served as governor of Tennessee during the Creek War and the War of 1812. When he received word of the massacre at Fort Mims, he authorized an army of militia under the command of Andrew Jackson to assist in putting down the Red Stick rebellion. He personally raised a significant amount of money, in excess of what the federal government had authorized, to support Tennessee troops in the field during the war. Although at one point Blount urged Jackson to give up his campaign after most of his army returned home when their enlistments expired, Blount did provide support to Tennessee's war efforts in defeating the Red Sticks. Counties in Tennessee and Alabama are named in his honor.

James Caller

A militia commander in Washington County, Mississippi Territory, James Caller organized the expedition that ambushed a Red Stick force at the Battle of Burnt Corn Creek. In the confusion following the battle, Caller became separated from his troops and got lost. He was not found until over two weeks later.

William Carroll

William Carroll served under Andrew Jackson during his campaigns against the Red Sticks and the British in the War of 1812. Born in Pittsburgh, he later settled in Tennessee and joined the militia. He quickly gained Jackson's favor, who appointed him brigade inspector. Carroll displayed noteworthy leadership and bravery in several battles, including Talladega, Emuckfau Creek, Enitachopco Creek and Horseshoe Bend. Carroll continued his service with Jackson during hostilities with Britain, playing an important role in the victory at New Orleans. He eventually served as governor of Tennessee. Carroll County, Tennessee, is named in his honor.

Joseph Carson

A commander in the Mississippi Territorial militia, Joseph Carson was one of the top-ranking military officials in the Tensaw District. At different times he was stationed at Fort Stoddert, Fort Glass and Fort Madison, but he is most well known for leading troops at the Battle of Holy Ground in December 1813.

Ferdinand L. Claiborne

A longtime military veteran and commander of the Mississippi Territorial militia, Ferdinand L. Claiborne was sent to the Tensaw area with his command in the summer of 1813. From his headquarters at Fort Stoddert, he oversaw preparations for defense of the region against Red Stick attack. He led the first organized offensive into Red Stick territory after the fall of Fort Mims, which culminated in the destruction of the Holy Ground. Suffering from poor health, he retired to his home in Natchez after the campaign.

William Charles Cole Claiborne

Few rose in the political ranks faster than William C.C. Claiborne, the governor of Louisiana during the War of 1812. A Tennessee Supreme Court justice at age twenty-one and a U.S. congressman at age twenty-five, he later became governor of the Mississippi Territory. Claiborne also oversaw the transfer of Louisiana to the United States following the Louisiana Purchase and served as governor of the Territory of Orleans prior to becoming governor of the state in 1812. Claiborne worked diligently to gather men and supplies to defend New Orleans, despite serious disagreements with Andrew Jackson. After the conflict, he served briefly in the U.S. Senate until his death in 1817. Counties in Tennessee and Mississippi are named in his honor.

Alexander Inglis Cochrane

British Vice Admiral Alexander Cochrane served as an officer in the British navy during the American Revolution, in several later campaigns against France and as governor of Guadalupe prior to the War of 1812. Appointed commander of the North American station in early 1814,

W.C.C. Claiborne. *From Benson J. Lossing,* The Pictorial Field-Book of the War of 1812.

Cochrane ordered several raids along the Chesapeake and helped plan the attacks on Washington, D.C., and Baltimore. He eventually became fixated on capturing the Gulf Coast and orchestrated the supplying of hostile Creeks and former slaves for the British offensive. He decided to attack New Orleans directly and was instrumental in the actions against that city. After the British defeat there, he orchestrated the capture of Fort Bowyer at Mobile Point.

John Cocke

A longtime politician, John Cocke led volunteers from East Tennessee in the Creek War. His failure to combine his force with that of Andrew Jackson out of fear that he might not achieve the glory he sought led to the unfortunate attacks on the Hillabee Creeks, who had previously surrendered to Jackson. Later in the war, Jackson had Cocke arrested for insubordination. Cocke later won acquittal, however, and remained active in politics throughout his life, serving in the U.S. House of Representatives for eight years.

John Coffee

John Coffee served with Andrew Jackson throughout the campaigns of the Creek War and the War of 1812. A longtime friend and associate of Old Hickory, Coffee settled in Middle Tennessee and had become a surveyor, merchant and developer by the time of the war. In Coffee's first tour with Jackson, he led a contingent of troops to Natchez in the Mississippi Territory. During Jackson's campaigns against the Red Sticks, he led mounted volunteers and participated in several encounters. He served as ranking commander on the field in the American victory at Tallushatchee, and he also played an important role in preventing the Red Sticks from escaping at Horseshoe Bend. Coffee also participated in the capture of Pensacola and the defense of New Orleans. Counties in Alabama, Georgia and Tennessee are named in his honor.

James Cornells

James Cornells had his plantation burned and his wife kidnapped after refusing to join the Red Sticks shortly before the Battle of Burnt Corn Creek in 1813. He attempted to warn the commander at Fort Mims of the approach of Red Sticks, but was ignored. After the war, he served at Fort Claiborne and had the opportunity to guard William Weatherford, who had come to the fort for protection after having threats made against him by angry residents.

Martha Crawley

Red Sticks captured Martha Crawley after their attack on a small settlement near the Duck River in Tennessee in May 1812. In the attack,

John Coffee. *From Benson J. Lossing,* The Pictorial Field-Book of the War of 1812.

led by Little Warrior, seven whites were killed. Treated poorly and believing that she would soon be killed, Crawley escaped from her captors near modern-day Tuscaloosa, reportedly through the assistance of a Native American woman and a white settler named Tandy Walker. Her accounts of the attack and her treatment at the hands of her captors caused alarm among white settlers and friendly Creeks and helped spur Agent Benjamin Hawkins to order that Little Warrior's band be brought to justice.

David Crockett

Legendary Davy Crockett of Tennessee volunteered to fight in the Creek War. He served mostly as a scout and teamster and saw little action, although he was present at the battle of Tallushatchee. After the war, he served several terms in the Tennessee legislature and was elected to the U.S. Congress. Crockett later fought for the independence of Texas from Mexico, dying at the Alamo in 1836. Crockett County, Tennessee, is named in his honor.

Samuel Dale

One of the most celebrated American heroes of the Creek War, Sam Dale witnessed Tecumseh's famous speech at Tuckaubatchee in 1811 and participated in the Battle of Burnt Corn Creek and the campaign against the Holy Ground. He is most famous for his role in the Canoe Fight, in which he and two others killed nine Red Stick warriors in the Alabama River.

Just prior to the Battle of New Orleans, Dale was hurriedly dispatched from Georgia to deliver an important message to General Andrew Jackson from the U.S. secretary of war. He arrived as the battle was raging. He later served in the Alabama legislature and subsequently spent his last years in Mississippi.

Sam Dale. *From J.F.H. Claiborne,* Life and Times of General Sam Dale, the Mississippi Partisan. *Courtesy of the Mississippi Department of Archives and History.*

Dale County, Alabama, and the community of Daleville, Mississippi, are named in his honor.

(His grave site, marked by a memorial to him and his accomplishments, is in Sam Dale Historical Site, located just off Highway 39, north of Meridian, Mississippi.)

Governor Peter Early

Peter Early succeeded David Mitchell as governor of Georgia in 1813, taking office just after open conflict between U.S. and Red Stick forces began. He remained in office for the duration of the war. Early County, Georgia, is named in his honor.

Thomas Flournoy

From his headquarters in New Orleans, Thomas Flournoy commanded the Seventh Military District, which included Louisiana, Tennessee and the Mississippi Territory, at the beginning of the Creek War. When General Thomas Pinckney was given overall command of the war effort against the Creeks, Flournoy nominally maintained control of all other military affairs in his district. He eventually resigned his post in frustration at not being granted total control of his territory.

John Floyd

John Floyd was selected by Georgia governor Peter Early in 1813 to lead an expedition against the Red Sticks by the militia of that state. He trained his army in central Georgia in the early fall of 1813 before leading them into Red Stick territory. From Fort Mitchell, he led troops in the campaigns that resulted in the battles of Autossee and Calabee Creek. He was subsequently sent to Savannah in anticipation of an expected British attack on that city, which never materialized. Floyd County, Georgia, is named in his honor.

Josiah Francis (Hillis Hadjo)

One of the most prominent of the Red Stick prophets and a veteran of several actions during the Creek War, Josiah Francis was one of many leading Creeks born to a Native American woman who had married a

John Floyd. *Courtesy of the Hargrett Rare Book and Manuscript Library/University of Georgia Libraries.*

European trader. Francis allegedly led the group of warriors that attacked Fort Sinquefield, and he probably played a significant role in the creation of the Red Stick stronghold at the Holy Ground. He continued to work with British military leaders on the Gulf Coast in a failed attempt to organize a Creek nation after the signing of the Treaty of Fort Jackson, even going so far as to visit with government officials in London. After living for a brief time in Nassau, he returned to Florida and settled along the Wakulla River. He was captured by Andrew Jackson during the First Seminole War and was hanged at St. Marks in April 1818.

Samuel Gibbs

British Major General Samuel Gibbs served as second in command to Edward Pakenham during the New Orleans campaign. During the main assault launched on January 8, 1815, Gibbs commanded the army's right wing, which was assigned to penetrate Jackson's line near the woods. His assault quickly disintegrated when the attack's lead regiment, the Forty-fourth Infantry, failed to bring forward the ladders and fascines necessary to scale the American rampart. Gibbs was mortally wounded at the head of his troops within twenty yards of the American line. A statue of him, along with his commanding officer Pakenham, now stands at St. Paul's Cathedral in London.

George Gilmer

A lieutenant in the Georgia militia, George Gilmer oversaw construction of Fort Peachtree, located in modern-day Atlanta. Gilmer later served as governor of Georgia. Gilmer County, Georgia, is named in his honor.

Benjamin Hawkins

President George Washington appointed Benjamin Hawkins as principal temporary agent for Indian affairs south of the Ohio River in 1796. He held the position until his death, becoming one of the most influential men in the Deep South during the era. From his agency on the Flint River in Georgia, he oversaw the administration of the federal government's program of "civilization" aimed at helping the Creeks to become yeoman farmers and thus—hopefully—more compatible with white society. Because of his position, Hawkins also became a key diplomat in disputes within the Creek Nation and those involving Creeks and white settlers. He tried hard to avert the war, urging rejection of Tecumseh's appeal to the Creeks and ordering the Red Sticks who murdered white settlers brought to justice. Greatly disheartened to see the conflict escalate into full-scale war with the United States, he looked for ways to peacefully end the war as it raged. He was appointed as one of the initial commissioners charged with negotiating a treaty ending the war with the Red Sticks, but he was

Benjamin Hawkins. *Courtesy of the North Carolina Department of Archives and History.*

later replaced by Andrew Jackson. Fort Hawkins was named in his honor. He died in Georgia in 1816.

(Hawkins is buried in Taylor County in a cemetery on Benjamin Hawkins Road just off State Highway 128. A memorial to him stands in the center of the town of Roberta, Georgia.) The city of Hawkinsville, Georgia, is named in his honor.

High Head Jim (Cusseta Hadjo or Jim Boy)

High Head Jim, a Red Stick prophet, was one of the earliest converts of Tecumseh. He was part of the group of warriors that was attacked on its way back from Pensacola at the first engagement of the war, the Battle of Burnt Corn Creek. He later participated in the attack on Fort Mims. In January 1814, he helped plan the surprise attack on Floyd's Georgia army at the Battle of Calabee Creek. Some sources state that he was killed in that battle, while some of the earlier writers to chronicle the Creek War indicate that he survived and later fought in the Seminole Wars.

Thomas Hinds

A native of Virginia, Thomas Hinds led the Mississippi Dragoons during hostilities against the Creeks and the British. Hinds's cavalry, composed of men from the Natchez District, guarded the frontier following the Red Stick attack on Fort Mims, but they were deemed undisciplined and dismissed by Seventh Military District commander General Thomas Flournoy. Hinds later led his command to New Orleans, where it provided valuable scouting assistance to Jackson, for which the general subsequently commended him. Following the conflict, Hinds worked with Jackson as one of the primary commissioners on the Choctaw Treaty of Doak's Stand in 1820 and also served on the commission that founded the city of Jackson, Mississippi. Hinds County, Mississippi, is named in his honor.

David Holmes

David Holmes served as governor of the Mississippi Territory during the Creek War. In charge of the territorial militia, he ordered General Ferdinand L. Claiborne to the Tensaw region in the summer of 1813 in anticipation of a confrontation with the Red Sticks. The last governor of the Mississippi Territory, he went on to serve as the first governor of the state of Mississippi. Holmes County, Mississippi, is named in his honor.

Hopoithle Miko

Hopoithle Miko was one of the most vocal Red Stick leaders. An elderly chief who hailed from the village of Tallassee, he was killed in the Battle of Autossee.

Sam Houston

Sam Houston served in the Tennessee militia in the Creek War before joining the Thirty-ninth Regiment of U.S. Infantry. He took part in the Battle of Horseshoe Bend, suffering several wounds that put him out of action for the remainder of the hostilities. Houston later served two terms in the U.S. Congress and as governor of Tennessee. Houston eventually became involved in Texas's fight for independence from Mexico, and he gained fame by leading troops to victory in the Battle of San Jacinto. He later served as president of the Republic of Texas and then as governor until secessionists removed him from office in 1861.

Andrew Jackson

Born into humble circumstances in South Carolina, Andrew Jackson eventually became the greatest spokesman for the interest of the American West, a victorious military general and president of the United States. Serving as major general of Tennessee militia, he led several campaigns during the Creek War. As much as any other single factor, his rugged determination and incredible willpower contributed to the Red Stick defeat. After securing millions of acres of Creek land for the United States via the Treaty of Fort Jackson, Jackson turned his attention to the nation's European threats. He first captured Pensacola from the Spanish and then later won one of this country's greatest military victories at the Battle of New Orleans. These successes eventually catapulted Old

Andrew Jackson. *Courtesy of the National Park Service.*

Hickory to the White House, where he served two terms. Numerous cities and counties across the nation have been named in his honor.

(The Hermitage, Jackson's home, is today operated as a museum that interprets his life and times. It is located twelve miles northeast of downtown Nashville, Tennessee.)

Thomas ap Catesby Jones

Thomas ap Catesby Jones served with the gunboat flotilla stationed at New Orleans in 1808 and helped guard the Gulf Coast against pirates and smugglers prior to the outbreak of the War of 1812. In September 1814, he participated in the attack on Jean Laffite and the Baratarians at their encampment at Grand Terre. A few months later, on December 14, Jones unsuccessfully led five American gunboats against forty British barges in the crucial battle for Lake Borgne. During the engagement, Jones was seriously wounded and eventually captured. Released in February 1815, Jones's career in the navy continued into the 1850s.

John Keane

British General John Keane led British troops assigned to attack New Orleans prior to the arrival of Edward Michael Pakenham. Faulted for bowing to the forceful personality of Admiral Alexander Cochrane during his brief period of command, he has also been roundly criticized for not pressing into the city immediately after landing. After relinquishing command, Keane was placed in charge of the British army's left wing during the main assault on January 8. During the attack, he fatefully ordered the Ninety-third Regiment to cross the field diagonally to assist General Samuel Gibbs. Keane survived the battle, despite being wounded severely, and went on to become governor of Jamaica and commander in chief in the West Indies.

Jean Laffite

Jean Laffite, whose life is surrounded by myth and legend, provided invaluable assistance to Andrew Jackson during the New Orleans campaign. Laffite and his brothers operated as smugglers and privateers from their base at Barataria on the Louisiana coast, where they became the target of U.S. authorities determined to shut them down in September 1814.

"Lafitte the Pirate." *Courtesy of the Historic New Orleans Collection (1983.123.9).*

Recognizing his value, British officials simultaneously approached Laffite to solicit his aid against the United States. Laffite reported this news to U.S. authorities and offered his services in the defense of New Orleans. Though the Louisiana legislature provided amnesty to Laffite and any Baratarian who offered to defend the city, Andrew Jackson at first refused to deal with him. He eventually relented, however, and Laffite and his men contributed crucial supplies and ammunition to Jackson's army, as well as advice on improving his defensive position. After the war, Laffite resumed his smuggling activities in Galveston. The exact circumstances of his death remain clouded in mystery.

John Lambert

British General John Lambert arrived in Louisiana in early January 1815 with reinforcements for the attack on New Orleans. British General Edward Pakenham placed Lambert in charge of the reserves for the main assault on January 8, but after Pakenham was killed and other British generals had been killed or wounded, he assumed control over the entire army. Instead of continuing the doomed attack, Lambert halted the offensive and soon afterward supervised the army's withdrawal from Louisiana. Before news arrived that the war had officially ended, he oversaw the land operations that resulted in the capture of Fort Bowyer in February 1815. Lambert later took part in the famous Battle of Waterloo.

Arsène Lacarrière Latour

Educated at the Paris Academy of the Fine Arts, engineer and architect Major Arsène Lacarrière Latour used his knowledge of the New Orleans area to help Andrew Jackson plan the defense of the city. He helped strengthen Jackson's defenses along the Rodriquez Canal, designed the American defenses on the west bank, helped improve the defenses at Fort St. Philip and provided Jackson with accurate information regarding the British landing and approach once their arrival became known. His friendship with Jean Laffite also helped lead Jackson to accept the Baratarian's aid. Ironically, Latour served as an agent for Spain after the war. His *Historical Memoir of the War in West Florida and Louisiana* remains one of the best firsthand accounts of the campaign.

William Lawrence

Major William Lawrence was ordered by General Andrew Jackson to defend Fort Bowyer, which guarded the entrance to Mobile Bay. Lawrence successfully repelled a combined British land and naval attack in mid-September 1814, which greatly boosted morale in the Gulf South

William Lawrence.
*Courtesy of Fort Morgan State
Historic Site.*

and earned high praise from Jackson himself. The British returned after their defeat at New Orleans, however, and launched a larger operation, landing several hundred troops with heavy artillery. On this occasion, Lawrence had no choice but to surrender in mid-February 1815. After the war, Lawrence remained in the army until 1831.

Little Prince (Tustunnuggee Hopoi)

A Lower Creek chief, Little Prince was an influential ally of the United States. Though too old for active military service during the war, he remained a powerful political ally during the conflict. He was one of the chiefs who persuaded Brigadier General John Floyd to come to the aid of the town of Coweta when it was besieged by Red Sticks, and he was present at the signing of the Treaty of Fort Jackson.

147

Little Warrior (Tustugnugachee)

A convert of Tecumseh, Little Warrior led the band of Red Stick warriors that followed the Shawnee leader north after his visit to Creek villages. On their return in the spring of 1812, they murdered several white settlers near the Duck River in Tennessee. The group was subsequently tracked down and executed after Benjamin Hawkins sent out a group of warriors charged with bringing them to justice.

Nicholas Lockyer

British navy Captain Nicholas Lockyer was part of the team sent to persuade Jean Laffite and his Baratarians to form an alliance against the United States. Lockyer is more famous for leading British gunboats to victory at Lake Borgne on December 14, 1814.

Lyncoya

Tennessee troops found Lyncoya, a Creek child named and adopted by Andrew Jackson, following the Battle of Tallushatchee. He lived with the Jacksons in Tennessee until his death at age seventeen.

Major Ridge

The son of a Cherokee and a Scottish trader, Cherokee Chief Major Ridge fought with the Americans in the Creek War and the War of 1812. Ridge favored his fellow Cherokees adapting the ways of the Americans. He became a wealthy planter himself, owning 250 acres of land, as well as a multitude of slaves. He preached against Tecumseh and served with Cherokee troops who campaigned against the Red Sticks. Taking the name "Major" when he earned that rank, Ridge figured prominently at the Battle of Horseshoe Bend, where he joined other Native Americans allied with U.S. forces and crossed the Tallapoosa River to attack Tohopeka from the rear. In the 1830s, Ridge migrated westward when the Cherokees were removed. Bitter Cherokees, upset at his role in giving up their ancestral lands, shot and killed him in 1839 in Indian Territory.

Major Ridge. *Courtesy of the Columbus Museum (1983.42).*

Don Mateo Gonzalez Manrique

The Spanish governor of West Florida, Don Mateo Gonzalez Manrique, made his headquarters in Pensacola during the Creek War and the War of 1812. Though initially hesitant to assist the Red Sticks during their conflict with the United States, he eventually supplied them with powder and other items. He solicited British assistance in the defense of Pensacola in 1814, when concerns arose about an American offensive against the town. Despite his efforts, he was ultimately forced to surrender the town to Andrew Jackson in November 1814.

William McIntosh. *Courtesy of the Columbus Museum (1983.39.2).*

William McIntosh (Tustunnugee Hutkee or White Warrior)

William McIntosh, the son of a British soldier and a Creek woman, as well as a cousin of Georgia Governor George M. Troup, was a leading Creek ally of the United States during the Creek War. McIntosh first became involved in the conflict while it was still a civil war among the Creeks, leading a group of men who executed the group of Red Sticks responsible for the murder of white settlers on the Duck River in February 1812. He later commanded Creek troops in support of U.S. forces on several occasions. He raided Red Stick villages in October 1813, assisted Floyd's troops at the Battle of Autossee and fought alongside Jackson's men at Horseshoe Bend. Commissioned a brigadier general in the U.S. Army for his service, McIntosh also fought in the First Seminole War. He was murdered in 1825 by a band of Creeks angered by his signing of the Treaty of Indian Springs, which ceded to the U.S. government all remaining Creek lands in Georgia.

(Portions of McIntosh's postwar plantation home, known as Lochau Talofau, is today part of McIntosh Reserve Park. The park is located along the Chattahoochee River near Carrollton, Georgia, and run by the Carroll County Recreation Department. The facility features McIntosh's grave site and a reproduction of his home.)

Peter McQueen

The son of a Scottish trader and a Creek woman, Peter McQueen became one of the principal Red Stick leaders. He participated in several battles during the Creek War, including the attack on Fort Mims and the Battles of Emuckfau Creek and Enitachopco Creek. He is most well known for leading the group of Red Sticks at the Battle of Burnt Corn Creek. After the Red Stick surrender, McQueen fled to Florida, where he continued in his effort to resist American expansion into former Creek territory. He fought against Jackson in the First Seminole War and died in south Florida shortly after its conclusion.

Menawa

Known as Great Warrior, Menawa became a follower of Tecumseh and a leading Red Stick chief. He led the Red Sticks at Horseshoe Bend, becoming one of the few defenders to escape the battlefield, despite being wounded seven times. He continued to fight against the encroachment of whites, as well as those Creeks willing to submit to American rule following the Creek War. He led a war party that killed Creek leader William McIntosh after he signed a treaty giving away Creek land. Menawa lived to see the final expulsion of the Creeks from the southeast and died in Indian Territory. The date of his death is unknown.

Menawa. *Courtesy of the Columbus Museum (1985.20).*

Homer V. Milton

An officer in the Third U.S. Infantry, Colonel Homer V. Milton commanded troops in General John Floyd's campaigns into Red Stick territory. Following the Battle of Calabee Creek, Milton held command at Fort Hull with a small detachment of troops, while Floyd led the remainder of his army back to Georgia. After receiving reinforcements,

Milton oversaw the construction of Forts Bainbridge and Decatur in an effort to create a line of supply stretching from the Chattahoochee to the Tallapoosa. Charged with stockpiling supplies for Andrew Jackson's army, he later moved his troops to the junction of the Coosa and Tallapoosa Rivers in April 1814 as Jackson approached that area after the Battle of Horseshoe Bend.

Samuel Mims

A prominent resident of the Tensaw region, Samuel Mims was a planter and ferry operator who had settled in the area prior to American jurisdiction. His plantation, one of the largest in the area, became the location of Fort Mims in the summer of 1813. Mims died during the Red Stick attack on the fortification.

David Mitchell

Governor David Mitchell of Georgia oversaw the strengthening of the state's militia as tensions with the Red Sticks escalated beginning in 1811. Once war between the United States and Great Britain was officially declared, Mitchell ordered the seizure of British vessels in the St. Mary's River. Fort Mitchell and Mitchell County, Georgia, are named in his honor.

Samuel Moniac

The half-Creek brother-in-law of William Weatherford, Samuel Moniac assisted the American military during the Creek War. His property was one of those destroyed by Red Sticks on their expedition to Pensacola in the summer of 1813. He is most well known for guiding the American army to the Holy Ground in December 1813.

Lemuel Montgomery

Major Lemuel Montgomery served in the Thirty-ninth U.S. regiment. A Nashville attorney whose grandfather had fought in the American Revolution, Montgomery was killed at Horseshoe Bend when he was shot while scaling the Red Stick fortification. Montgomery County, Alabama, is named in his honor.

Lemuel Montgomery statue, downtown Montgomery, Alabama. *Photo courtesy of authors.*

David Morgan

A Louisiana politician prior to the war, General David Morgan commanded Louisiana militia during the New Orleans campaign. Morgan is most remembered for unsuccessfully leading the American force charged with defending the west bank of the Mississippi River on January 8, 1815.

Daniel Newnan

Daniel Newnan commanded a regiment of infantry in Brigadier General John Floyd's army during its campaigns into Red Stick territory in 1813 and 1814. A veteran of the unsuccessful "Patriot War" designed to seize Spanish Florida for the United States, Newnan was an established and respected leader by the time Floyd organized his army. He commanded troops at both Autossee and Calabee Creek, where he was wounded three times. The city of Newnan, Georgia, is named in his honor.

Edward Nicolls

British Major Edward Nicolls worked to secure Creek allies for the British cause during the War of 1812. Beginning in August 1814, he provided supplies, food and training to Creek refugees in Spanish West Florida and oversaw construction of a fort at Prospect Bluff, north of present-day Apalachicola. He transferred his command to Pensacola to assist the Spanish in fending off American encroachment, and was subsequently severely wounded in the British attack on Fort Bowyer at Mobile Point. After the war, Nicolls unsuccessfully fought for enforcement of Article IX of the Treaty of Ghent, which he believed would restore Creek lands.

Edward Michael Pakenham

General Edward Pakenham, the brother-in-law of the famed Duke of Wellington, commanded the British army that attempted to capture New Orleans. Having earned acclaim in the various wars against France, and especially in the Peninsular Campaign of 1809–14, Pakenham was given command of the North American British army after the death of Robert Ross. Pakenham arrived after the British forces landed opposite Andrew Jackson's fortified line, and though mortified at the horrible

"Major General The Honorable Sir Edward Michael Pakenham." *Courtesy of the Historic New Orleans Collection (1991.34.30).*

British position, he determined to move forward with plans to capture the important city. Pakenham was killed in the main assault on the Rodriguez Canal on January 8, 1815, and his remains were carried back to England. A life-size statue of him, and his second in command, Samuel Gibbs, now stands at St. Paul's Cathedral in London.

Daniel Patterson

Naval officer Daniel Patterson, who joined the navy at age thirteen, served during the Quasi-War against France, against the Barbary pirates and in the occupation of Baton Rouge in 1810 before receiving command of the New Orleans station in July 1813. He led the successful attack against Jean Laffite and the Baratarians at Grand Terre in September 1814. He authorized the gunboat fleet that monitored Lake Borgne and personally commanded the gunboat *Carolina* during its assault on the British on December 23, 1814. During the British main assault on Jackson's line on January 8, 1815, Patterson commanded a battery on the west bank. After the war, he commanded the famous USS *Constitution* in the Mediterranean and served as commandant of the Washington Navy Yard.

Hugh Pigot

Sent by British Admiral Alexander Cochrane, Captain Hugh Pigot was the first to make contact with Native Americans to secure their support for a British offensive on the Gulf Coast during the War of 1812. Pigot's optimistic reports after his arrival near the Apalachicola River in May 1814 helped convince Admiral Alexander Cochrane that the Gulf Coast was indeed vulnerable and that the British could rely on these newfound Native American allies.

Thomas Pinckney

Thomas Pinckney commanded the Sixth Military District, which included Georgia and the Carolinas, at the beginning of the Creek War. In November 1813, he was given overall command of the U.S. war effort against the Creeks. This was largely due to the fact that it was easier to maintain effective communications between Washington and his base in Charleston than New Orleans, headquarters of the Seventh Military District, in which most of the fighting actually took place. He served in this capacity through the end of hostilities in the summer of 1814, when he received an appointment to serve as one of the initial commissioners charged with negotiating a treaty with the Creeks. He was later replaced as commissioner by Andrew Jackson.

Pushmataha

Pushmataha, a Choctaw chief, was among the most prominent anti–Red Stick Native American leaders. He became one of the most vocal critics of Tecumseh during his visit to the southern tribes, and worked continually to counter his influence and maintain the neutrality of the Choctaws prior to the outbreak of the war. Following the attack on Fort Mims, he led a group of warriors in Claiborne's campaign against the Holy Ground. The leading Choctaw chief for over two decades, Pushmataha represented his tribe in a wide variety of negotiations between the Choctaws and the United States, including the landmark Treaty of Doak's Stand (1820), which ceded over five million acres of Choctaw land to the federal government in exchange for land west of the Mississippi River. He died in 1824 in Washington, D.C., where he had gone to negotiate enforcement of the terms of the treaty relating to the Choctaw's new lands. He was buried with full military honors as an officer in the United States Army.

(Pushmataha is buried in the Congressional Cemetery in Washington, D.C.)

Robert Rennie

British Colonel Robert Rennie led two attacks during the campaign for New Orleans. He nearly succeeded in turning Jackson's left flank during the British foray on December 28, 1814. During the main British assault on January 8, Rennie led a column of nearly one thousand men that attacked and captured Jackson's advanced redoubt located near the river, but he was shot and killed as he climbed atop the main fortification.

Gilbert C. Russell

Gilbert C. Russell commanded the Third Regiment of U.S. Infantry during the war. He participated in Claiborne's campaign against the Holy Ground in December 1813, and in February 1814, he led a brief excursion up the Cahaba River to destroy Red Stick settlements. Russell County, Alabama, is named in his honor.

John Strother

John Strother served as a topographical engineer in Andrew Jackson's army and designed several of the army's fortifications and supply bases.

Fort Strother was named in his honor. Strother recommended that allied Native Americans wear white plumes in their hats to distinguish them from their Red Stick foes.

Tecumseh

Born in modern day Ohio, Tecumseh became a leading figure in Native American resistance to white settlement in the first decade of the nineteenth century by promoting the idea of an Indian Confederacy as a way to ensure the survival of native tribes. He traveled southward in the summer and fall of 1811 to rally the Chickasaws, Choctaws and Creeks to his cause. He was largely unsuccessful except with a portion of the Upper Creeks, many of whom he addressed at their annual council meeting at Tuckaubatchee. His already receptive audience became even more supportive when his prophecies regarding the appearance of a comet and the occurrence of an earthquake seemed to be fulfilled shortly after his visit. Tecumseh returned north and became an ally of the British in the War of 1812, taking part in several important actions against U.S. forces in the Detroit River region. He was killed in the Battle of the Thames on October 5, 1813.

Jett Thomas

Jett Thomas commanded the Baldwin Volunteer Artillery in General John Floyd's army, serving with distinction at the Battles of Autossee and Calabee Creek. An architect who had built the Georgia state capitol in Milledgeville prior to the war, Thomas served as Floyd's chief engineer. Thomas County, Georgia, and the county seat of Thomasville are named in his honor.

(His grave is in Memory Hill Cemetery in Milledgeville, Georgia.)

William Thornton

British Colonel William Thornton was already a veteran of the War of 1812 before the campaign for New Orleans. Most notably, he had been wounded while leading troops at the Battle of Bladensburg in August 1814, the British victory that led to the burning of Washington, D.C. He then led many of the first troops that landed unopposed on Louisiana soil on December 23, 1814. After gaining a foothold only a few miles from New Orleans, he urged General John Keane to press forward into the city immediately, but to no avail. General Edward Pakenham assigned Thornton responsibility for capturing the American position on the west bank as part of the main assault on January 8, 1815. Unfortunately for the British, Thornton's troops were delayed in crossing the river and made their successful attack, in which he was again wounded, after the main assault on the east bank had already failed. He continued his military career after the war, obtaining the rank of lieutenant general, but he never fully recovered physically or psychologically from the wounds he obtained during the war. He committed suicide in 1840.

Harry Toulmin

Harry Toulmin served as judge of the Superior Court of the Tombigbee District in the Mississippi Territory during the Creek War. The area's most prominent federal official, he was intimately familiar with many of the most important developments of the war in the region. His prolific writings, especially his recording of events surrounding the fall of Fort Mims, have become some of the best sources of information on the initial stages of the Creek War. As a leading citizen of the Mississippi Territory, he played a role in many significant events, including the arrest of Aaron Burr in 1807. He also became the first person to codify the laws of the states of Mississippi and Alabama.

Gabriel Villeré

During the New Orleans campaign, Major Gabriel Villeré of the Louisiana militia was ordered by Andrew Jackson to block the canals and waterways that connected the Mississippi River to the various lakes in the region. Failing to comply with those orders, Villeré was caught on the porch of his father's (General Jacques Villeré was commander of the entire Louisiana militia) plantation when British troops arrived on December 23, 1814. Gabriel Villeré managed to escape his captors and reported to Jackson that British troops had landed and were mere miles from the city. After the conflict, Villeré was acquitted during a court-martial trial, and his father eventually became governor of Louisiana.

William Weatherford grave site. *Photo courtesy of authors.*

Paddy Walsh

Paddy Walsh was one of the principal Red Stick prophets and one of the leaders of the attack on Fort Mims. He led warriors who attacked General John Floyd's rear guard after the Battle of Autossee and directed one of the best-planned Red Stick attacks of the war at the Battle of Calabee Creek.

William Weatherford (Red Eagle)

Half Scottish and half Creek, William Weatherford joined the Red Stick cause and went on to become one of its most famous and influential leaders. He helped plan the attacks on Fort Mims and the American encampment at Calabee Creek, and he famously escaped capture at the Battle of the Holy Ground by leaping his horse into the Alabama River.

In the aftermath of the devastating Red Stick defeat at Horseshoe Bend, he entered Fort Jackson alone and voluntarily surrendered himself to General Andrew Jackson. Though his capture had been one of the top goals of the American military, Jackson pardoned him out of respect for his display of bravery on the condition that he use his influence to persuade remaining bands of Red Sticks to lay down their arms. He spent his final years on his plantation in southern Alabama, where he died in 1824.

(The William Weatherford Monument, which contains the graves of Weatherford and his mother, is located on County Road 84 in northern Baldwin County, Alabama.)

James Wilkinson

As head of the Seventh Military District, General James Wilkinson led the American force that seized Fort Charlotte and the disputed territory of West Florida from Spain in April 1813. Later in the War of 1812, he led two unsuccessful campaigns against the British on the Canadian border. Wilkinson's career included service in the Revolutionary War, as governor of the Louisiana Territory and as a high-ranking officer in the U.S. Army. Wilkinson was a controversial and widely unpopular figure who secretly worked as a spy for Spain for many years.

John Williams

Knoxville lawyer John Williams served as colonel of the U.S. Thirty-ninth Regiment during the Creek War. Earlier, he had led volunteers against the Seminoles in 1812. His regular troops provided the backbone of Andrew Jackson's reorganized army, which defeated the Red Sticks at Horseshoe Bend. Fort Williams was named in his honor.

Original Documents

This chapter contains transcriptions of a variety of types of private and public correspondence written before, during and after the war. These documents assist in the understanding of the conflict by providing firsthand accounts of many of its most important events. While some transcriptions have been edited slightly for brevity, we present them with their original spelling and punctuation.

1. Excerpt from Tecumseh's speech at Tuckaubatchee
2. Captain J.P. Kennedy's report following the Battle of Fort Mims
3. Jeremiah Austill's account of the Canoe Fight
4. General Ferdinand Claiborne's letter following the Battle of the Holy Ground
5. James Tait's accounts of the Battles of Autossee and Calabee Creek
6. General Andrew Jackson's letter following the Battle of Tallushatchee
7. General Andrew Jackson's letter to his wife following the Battle of Horseshoe Bend
8. Admiral Alexander Cochrane's letter to the Creek Nation
9. General Andrew Jackson's letter following the Battle of New Orleans
10. The Treaty of Fort Jackson

1. Excerpt From Tecumseh's Speech at Tuckaubatchee

Oh, Muscogees! Brethren of my mother! Brush from your eyelids the sleep of slavery, and strike for vengeance and your country! The red men have fallen as the leaves now fall. I hear their voices in those aged pines. Their tears drop from the weeping skies. Their bones bleach on the hills of Georgia. Will no son of those brave men strike the pale face and quiet these complaining ghosts? Let the white race perish! They seize your land;

they corrupt your women; they trample on the bones of your dead! Back whence they came, upon a trail of blood, they must be driven! Back—aye, back into the great water whose accursed waves brought them to our shores! Burn their dwellings—destroy their stock—slay their wives and children, that the very breed may perish. War now! War always! War on the living! War on the dead! Dig their very corpses from their graves. The red man's land must give no shelter to a white man's bones!

As recorded from eyewitness accounts by J.F.H. Claiborne in *Mississippi as a Province, Territory and State with Biographical Notices of Eminent Citizens* (Jackson, MS: Power and Barksdale, 1880).

2. Captain J.P. Kennedy to Brigadier General Ferdinand L. Claiborne

Following the Battle of Fort Mims

Mount Vernon, September 9, 1813

Sir,

Agreeable to your order of the eighth we proceeded with all possible dispatch to Mims' fort on Tensaw to examine the fatal field of battle and the situation of the country. We found the whole of the rich Tensaw settlements a perfect desert; the hand of destruction has passed over it, the remains of Major Beasley, our fellow citizens and brother soldiers still unburied next called our attention. You expect a faithful detail and correct picture of the scene. Language cannot convey it nor the pencil of the painter delineate it. Suffice it to say, that the small command of eight men who only accompanied us, touched by the affecting circumstances, we resolved to see the remains of our slaughtered fellow citizens and brother soldiers, perhaps the last human office that ever we could render to the unfortunate and brave Major Beasley, his slaughtered citizens and soldiers. Some felt the touch of nature for their relations, others for their friends, and all lamented the disaster of war, and the wretched lot of human nature. Our little band marched from the landing in gloomy solitude to the fort. The place presented an awful spectacle, and the tragical fate of our friends increased the horror of the scene. Our business was to find our friends and number the dead, an awful and melancholy duty. At the east gate of the stockade lay Indian, negroes, men, women, and children in one promiscuous ruin; within the gate lay the brave unfortunate Beasley, he was behind the same, and was killed, as was said in attempting to shut it. On the left within the stockade, we found forty-five more, women and children in one heap, they were stripped of their cloths without distinction of age or sex. All were scalped, and the females of every age were most barbarously and savage-like butchered, in a manner which neither decency nor language can convey. Women pregnant, were cut open and their children's heads tomahawked. This was supposed to be the fatal spot where the few, who escaped the general massacre, made their last efforts and perished in the attempt.

The large house within the fort was burned to ashes, and the ruins covered with human bones, the number and the persons who there perished could not be ascertained. The plains and the woods around were covered with dead bodies in some places thinly scattered, in others lying in heaps, as the men happened to fall in flight, or in a body resisted to the last. The result of the awful duty assigned us was that we found twenty Indians and two chiefs, nine negroes, thirty children, two infants, seventy-one men and twenty-nine women. The Indians were dressed in soldiers' clothes no doubt for the purpose of disguise, we distinguished them from the whites by their ears and the cut of the hair, the two chiefs were carried from the fort and buried by covering them with rails, and from what we could discover considerable more Indians were carried off and buried by their friends. All the houses within the fort were consumed by fire, except the blockhouse and part of the pickets unburned. While employed in this duty, our hearts were torn with contending passions, by turns with grief and burning with revenge. The soldier and officer with one voice called on divine providence to revenge the death of our murdered friends, and despaired of this unhappy country deserted by its inhabitants, seeking an asylum in some more happy clime, where the Peace Songs and Civil War stories will not delude the people and deceive those who are appointed to govern and protect them.

Your servant,
J.P. Kennedy, Captain and Brigade Major

Pickett Papers, Alabama Department of Archives and History.

3. Jeremiah Austill's Account of the Canoe Fight

On the 12th of Nov. 1813, Capt. Dale proposed an expedition upon the Alabama & was joined by Capt. Jones, making the party consist in all of 72 men. We struck the river above Jamestown where we procured two canoes &

spent the night in the cane without fire. The next morning Dale, with all but 8 (eight) men started up on the East bank leaving me in command of the boats, to keep parallel with the land force. On reaching Bayly's farm a halt was made. Dale came on board, crossed to the farm & searched the same, finding plenty of fresh tracks. Returning, he started for Randon's plantation where I was to meet him. Soon after starting I discovered a boat descending with ten (10) Indians in it, who tacked about seeing us. We gave chase immediately & gained fast upon them. One half mile above they ran up Randons Creek, into the Cane. Soon after Dale & Jones met a party of Indians in the Cane, crossing the Creek. Dale killed the one in front. The Indians then dropped their packs, a fire was kept up for a few minutes after which the Indians fled in the Cane.

As the firing ceased I pushed on up to the Landing, Where the land party soon after arrived—This was Randon's Landing, below Jim Correls Landing or ferry. Capt. Jones crossed over with his men & all of Dale's Company, except twelve (12) men, namely Dale, Maj. Creagh, Smith Brady, Myself & Six others. We were roasting potatoes & beef taken up at the Creek, where the fight took place. Just as we were taking the potatoes from the fire a large body of Indians was discovered marching off on either side to surround us. We ran to the bank of the river & neither of the canoes had returned, the small one was on the way over. Just then we discovered a large Canoe descending with eleven Indians in it.

As we were in a three acre field, we ascended the bank about twenty yds. & commenced firing, on the Indians in the boat, which was returned by them for several rounds, when two of them crept—met & made for the shore, some sixty or eighty yds above us & above the mouth of a small creek. Smith & I ran up to kill them & were followed by Creagh, who found us up to the waist in mud. We scuffled out & tho very heavy reached the place in time. We had to stand on the slope of the bank from which I slipped & fell into the river.

Just in front of one of them, both were carrying their guns above water. Smith fired & killed one, while the other sprang up & presented his gun at Smith as he ascended the bank, passing over my gun. I was after him, but ere I could recover my gun, he was in the Cane. I pursued him some forty yds for an open space to shoot & was just within four feet of a place when a gun was fired within thirty feet of me, the load passing just over my head. I turned to fire on the offender & Creagh was Just ascending the bank of the creek as I was passing in the Cane—supposing me to be an Indians & by this means my Indian escaped. We returned to Smith & descended the river on the turn of the back to our squad. Dale in the meantime called to Capt. Jones to send over the large canoe to capture the Indian boat. Eight men started over, but when within *fifty yds, the man in front rose up so as to see the number who were lying down loading their guns. He called to the paddler to back out as there were so many Indians in the boat, whereupon they retreated, the small boat having reached us, paddled by an old Negro named Caesar. During the interval I ordered Brady to ascend the second bank to see if a land party of Indians were closing in upon us. He crawled up but seeing no Indians he mounted a pile of earth, whereupon some guns were discharged at him, shooting the breech of his gun off. With one bound, he was in our midst swearing it was too hot up there for him. Dale then proposed to Smith & I to board the boat. Dale then leaped down some ten feet, Smith & I following. We entered the boat in the same order placing one in the boat. We ran out some twenty yds below the Indians. They rose up & we all attempted to fire. Dale's rifle & my own missed fire from the wetting of our priming getting into the boat & the rolling of the boat caused Smith to miss his aim. Dale then ordered Caesar to paddle up in a hurry & upon approaching their boat, the chief & I exchanged blows with our guns. Catching the end of his, I drew him up to me within reach of Smith & Dale who fought him down. Dale broke the barrel of his gun into & Smith caught the muzzle with which he fought out the battle.—Dale getting Smith's gun with which he made his blows. I used the Chief's gun.*

As we were running up broadside I had two upon me at one time until Dale got in the Indian boat & placed himself opposite Smith. On reaching the last two, one of them knocked me down with a War Club—falling across their boat & holding on to the club until I recovered my feet, one in each boat—a scuffle ensued for the club, which I gained & with which I knocked him overboard, the one in my rear, having been killed by Dale & Smith. So ended the battle. We then started back, with old Caesar paddling & Smith holding the boats together, while Dale and I threw the Indians overboard as there were yet eight bodies left in the boat. When about half way, a ball passed through the boat & on looking up we saw three Indians on the second bank Just above our ____[?] men, then under the first bank the second on taking rest on a stump. We stood up sideways & his ball struck the water, short of the boat—he at last took his seat—with a large bored rifle. I could see along the barrel & felt sure he would hit me. I drew myself up & stopped breathing—his ball passed within an inch of my abdomen, much to my relief. As we were approaching the same shore, the Indians retired to their main body of 280 (two hundred & eighty) Indians. We reached our nine comrades & crossed over to the west, without the Indians knowing it.

Alabama Department of Archives and History, SPR 55.

4. General Ferdinand Claiborne to Secretary of War John Armstrong

Following the Battle of the Holy Ground

Fort Claiborne, eighty-five miles above Fort Stoddert, January 1, 1814

Sir,

On the 13th ultimo, I marched a detachment from this post with the view of destroying the towns of the inimical Creek Indians on the Alabama, above the mouth of the Cahaba. After having marched about eighty miles, from the best information I could obtain, I was within thirty miles of a town, newly erected on ground called Holy, occupied by a large body of the enemy, under command of Weatherford, the half breed chief, who was one of those who commanded the Indians that destroyed the garrison at Mims in August last, and who has committed many depredations on the frontier inhabitants. I immediately caused a stockade to be erected for the security of the heavy baggage and sick. On the morning of the 23rd the troops resumed their line of march chiefly through woods, without a track to guide them. When near the town, on the morning of the 23rd, my disposition for attack was made. The troops advanced in three columns. With the entire column I advanced myself, ordering Lester's guards and Welle's troop of dragoons to act as a corps of reserve. About noon the right column, composed of twelve months volunteers, commanded by Colonel Joseph Carson, came in view of the town called Eccanachaca, or Holy Ground, and was immediately vigorously attacked by the enemy, who were apprised of our approach, and had chosen their field of action.

Before the center, commanded by Lieutenant Colonel Russell with a part of the 3rd Regiment of United States infantry and mounted militia riflemen, on the left column, which was composed of militia and a party of Choctaws, under Pushmataha, commanded by Major Smoot, of militia, who were ordered to charge, could come generally into action, the enemy were repulsed, and were flying in all directions, many of them casting away their arms. Thirty of the enemy were killed, and, judging from every appearance, many were wounded. The loss on our part was one corporal killed, and one ensign, two sergeants, one corporal and two privates wounded.

A pursuit was immediately ordered; but from the nature of the country, nothing was effected. The town was nearly surrounded by swamps and deep ravines, which rendered our approach difficult, and facilitated the escape of the enemy. In the town we found a large quantity of provision and immense property of various kinds, which the enemy, flying precipitately, were obliged to leave behind, and which, together with two hundred houses, were destroyed. They had barely time to remove their women and children across the Alabama, which runs near where the town stood. The next day was occupied in destroying a town, consisting of sixty houses, eight miles higher up the river, and in taking and destroying the enemy's boats. At the town last destroyed was killed three Indians of some distinction. The town first destroyed was built since the commencement of hostilities, and was established as a place of security for the inhabitants of several villages. The leader Weatherford, Francis, and the Choctaw Sinquistar's son, who were principal prophets, resided here. Three Shawnees were among the slain.

Colonel Carson of the volunteers, Lieutenant Colonel Russell, of the Third Regiment United States infantry, and Major Smoot, of the militia, greatly distinguished themselves. The activity and zeal of the assistant deputy quartermaster general, Captain West, and my brigade major, Kennedy, merit the approbrium of government. I was much indebted to my aide-de-camp, Lieutenant Calvit, of volunteers, to Robeson, of the Third Regiment, and Major Caller, of militia, who acted as my aids on that day, for the promptness and ability with which they performed their several duties. The officers of the different corps behaved handsomely, and are entitled to distinction. Courage animated every countenance, and each vied with the other in rendering service.

I have taken the liberty of communicating to you directly, in consequence of the distant station of the general commanding the district, and also for the purpose of forwarding to you the enclosed original document which was found in the house of Weatherford. It shows particularly the conduct of the Spaniards towards the American government. The Third Regiment has returned to this place, and volunteers are on the march to Mount Vernon, near Fort Stoddert, for the purpose of being paid off and discharged, their terms of service having generally expired.

I have the honor to be, and etc.,
Ferdinand L. Claiborne
Brigadier General of Volunteers

John Brannan, *Official Letters of the Military and Naval Officers of the United States, During the War with Great Britain in the years 1812, 13, 14, and 15* (Washington, D.C.: Way and Gideon, 1823).

5. Journal of James A. Tait for the Year 1813

Containing Accounts of the Battles of Autossee and Calabee Creek

Account of the Battle of Autossee:

Some particulars of the battle on the Tallapoosa, fought on the 29th November under the command of General Floyd on our part. After three days march, the army, (1800 strong, including 500 Indians, besides 800 infantry, 200 cavalry, 200 riflemen and an artillery company of 100 men); encamped on the night of the 28th within eight miles of the Autossee town the place of battle. The next morning it marched so soon as to exhibit itself to the surprised and astonished Indians, about half way between daybreak and sunrise; at this period the contest commenced. Then, for the first time, we heard to resound on the remote banks of the Tallapoosa the dreadful noise of contending armies, never before did the limpid waters receive the tinge of human blood. The battle lasted two and a half or three hours. Nine of our men were slain on the fields, some say 100, some 200 and some 300 of the enemy. They retired behind the bank of the river and as they were shot rolled into the stream, and were also derived into it to prevent the efforts of the scalping knife. Some were killed in swimming across. It is supposed that between 1500 and 2000 of the enemy were engaged. Three of our wounded died after the conflict. Captains King, Little, and Morris were wounded. The brave Adjutant General Newnan and our brave and respected General Floyd, the latter having his knee pan broken, the former slightly in the leg. There were eighteen rounds of cannon fired shattering their miserable huts to pieces. The enemy stuck close to their houses before this, through holes which were cut out, firing upon us. When the big guns were let loose, they left their huts and scampered like so many wild ants, some parts of their conduct were truly strange, several of them remained in their houses quite passive during the battle, suffering themselves to be slain without resistance. Whether was this the effects of prophetic influence? There were but few of them who were not in a state of complete nudity. Whether from necessity or choice I cannot pretend to say. Why from the former? For where are their dressed deer skins? Why from the latter? For it was very cold. Two of their kings shard the fatal portion of many of their subjects. The old Tallassee king mounted a horse from whence he encouraged his warriors by frequent waivings of his war club, himself firing upon us, at intervals with his rifle. Being discovered by Captain Thomas, of the artillery, a cannon was directed towards him—charged with grape shot, one of which took effect in the neck of the brave old king; the club no longer felt the grasp of its war possessor.

Account of the Battle of Calabee Creek:

[T]he 26th we struck up the line of march early. Moved on about a mile and a half, struck off to the right into the woods, marched a mile, halted, faced about (the General having resolved to send back the wagons by which we were retarded) and marched back about three sevenths of a mile to the ground on which we encamped. At this camp the next morning the 27th we were attacked by the enemy, before day about one half hour; the battle raged for about three quarters of an hour when we charged upon them, drove them off, and killed several. Captain Hamilton's troops of horse slew fifteen in the charge. Our loss was seventeen killed and 132 in wounded. The number slain on the part of the enemy was ascertained to be about fifty. The camp was too small, the men being two deep in line when drawn up to our camp. At the time of attack we had to draw in behind our fires, which made the lines still closer. If the camp had been fortified, to do which we had ample time, we should not have had twenty men in killed and wounded. We were on the battle ground six days in an entrenched camp. Thence moved down to Fort Hull on the first day of February. Thence on our return march for home on the 16th February. We reached the Ocmulgee on the 26th. Thence were conveyed to Milledgeville and not discharged until the 7th March.

Peter A. Brannan, ed., "Journal of James Tait for the Year 1813," *Alabama Historical Quarterly* 2 (Winter 1940): 431–40.

6. General Andrew Jackson to Governor Willie Blount

Following the Battle of Tallushatchee

Ten island Camp,
November 4, 1813

His Excellency W. Blount,
We have retaliated for the destruction of Fort Mims. On the 2d inst. I detached Genl. John Coffee with a part of his Brigade of Cavalry and mounted riflemen

to destroy *Tallishatchee*, where a considerable force of the hostile Creeks was concentrated. The General executed this order in stile. A hundred and eighty six of the enemy were found dead on the field and eighty taken prisoners; forty of whom have been brought here. In the number left, there is a sufficiency, but slightly wounded, to take care of those who are badly.

I have to regret that five of my brave fellows have been killed, and about thirty wounded—some badly, but none, I hope mortally. Both officers and men behaved with the utmost bravery and deliberation. Captains Smith, Bradley and Winston are wounded slightly. No officer is killed. So soon as Genl. Coffee makes his Report I shall enclose it. If we had a sufficient supply of provisions, we should in a very short time, accomplish the object of the expedition.

I have the honor to be etc…

P.S. Seventeen Cherokees under the command of Col. Brown acted with great bravery in the action.
Two of Chennubby's men and Jim Fife (of the Natchez tribe) also distinguished themselves.

John Spencer Bassett, ed., *Correspondence of Andrew Jackson*, Vol. 1 (Washington, D.C. 1926), 341.

7. General Andrew Jackson to His Wife Following the Battle of Horseshoe Bend

Fort Williams, April 1, 1814

My dear,
I returned to this place on yesterday three o'clock P.M. from an excursion against Tohopeka, and about one hour after had the pleasure of receiving your affectionate letter of the 22nd ultimo.

I have the pleasure to state to you that on the 27th march that I attacked and have destroyed the whole combined force, of the Newyokas, Oakfuskas, Hillabays, Fish ponds, Acacas, and Ufalee, Tribes. The carnage was dreadful. They had possessed themselves of one of the most military sites, I ever saw, which they had as strongly fortified with logs, across the neck of a bend. I endeavored, to levell the works with my cannon, but in vain. The balls passed thro the works without shaking the wall, but carrying destruction *to the enemy behind it. I had sent Genl Coffee across the river, with his horse and Indians who had completely surrounded the bend, which cut off their escape, and the Cherokees effected a landing on the extreme point of the bend with about one hundred and fifty of Genl Coffees Brigade, including Capt. Russles spy company. The Battle raged, about two hours, when I found those engaged in the interior of the bend, were about to be overpowered, I ordered, the charge and carried the works, by storm—after which they Indians took possession of the river bank, and part of their works raised with brush getting into the interior of the bend—and it was dark before we finished killing them. I ordered the dead bodies of the Indians to be counted, the next morning, and exclusive of those buried in their watry grave, who were killed in the [river] and who after being wounded plunged into it, there were counted, five hundred and fifty seven. from the report of Genl Coffee and the officers surrounding the bend, they are of opinion, that there could not be less than three hundred, killed in the river, who sunk and could not be counted. I have no doubt, but at least Eight hundred and fifty were slain. About twenty who had hid under the bank in the water, made their Escape in the night, one of whom was taken the next morning who gives this account, that they were all wounded from which I believe about 19 wounded Indians alone escaped. We took about three hundred and fifty prisoners, women and children and three warriors. What effect this will produce upon those infatuated and deluded people I cannot yet say. having destroyed at Tohopeka, three of their princip[al] prophets leaving but two in the nation—having tread their holy ground as the[y] termed it, and destroyed all their chiefs and warriors on the Tallapoosee river above the big bend, it is probable they may now sue for peace. Should they not (If I can be supplied with provisions) I will give them, with the permission of heaven the final stroke at the hickory ground, in a few days we have lost in killed of the whites 26, and one hundred and seven wounded. Amongst the former is Major Montgomery who bravely fell on the walls, and of the latter Colo. Carroll, slightly—our friends all safe, and Jack you may say to Mrs. Caffery reallised all my expectations he fought bravely, and killed an Indian. every officer and man did his duty. The 39th distinguished themselves and so did the militia, who stormed the works with them. There never was more heroism or roman courage displayed. I write in haste surrounded with a pressure of business, and a little fatigued. I will write you again before I leave this place. For the present I can only add, that I hope shortly to put an end to the war and return to your arms, kiss my little Andrew for me, tell him I have warriors bow and quiver for him. Give my compliments to all my friends, and cheer up the spirits of your Sister*

Cafferry, and receive my sincere prayers for your health and happiness until I return. affectionately adieu.

John Spencer Bassett, ed., *Correspondence of Andrew Jackson*, Vol. 1 (Washington, D.C., 1926), 492–94.

8. Admiral Alexander Cochrane's Letter to the Creek Nation

Given at the Start of the Campaign for New Orleans

To the Great and Illustrious Chiefs of the Creek and other Indian Nations

Hear!—O Ye Brave Chiefs and Warriors of the Creek and Other Indian Nations.

The Great King George, our beloved Father, has long wished to assuage the sorrows of his warlike Indian Children, and to assist them in regaining their Rights and Possessions from their base and perfidious oppressors.

The trouble our Father has had in conquering his Enemies beyond the great waters, he has brought to a glorious conclusion; and Peace is again restored amongst all Nations of Europe.

The desire therefore which he has long felt of. assisting you, and the assurance which he has given you of his powerful protection, he has now chosen us his Chiefs by Sea and Land to carry into effectual execution.

Know then, O Chiefs and Warriors, that in obedience to the Great Spirit which directs the soul of our mighty Father, we come with a power which it were vain for all People of the United States to attempt to oppose—Behold the great waters covered with our Ships, from which will go forth an Army of Warriors as numerous as the whole Indian Nation; inured to the toils and hardships of war—accustomed to triumph over all opposition—the constant favorites of Victory.

The same principle of justice which led our Father to wage a war of twenty years in favor of the oppressed Nations of Europe, animates him now in support of his Indian Children. And by the efforts of his Warriors, he hopes to obtain for them the restoration of those lands of which the People of the Bad Spirit have basely robbed them.

We promised you by our Talk of last June, that great fleets and armies were coming to attack our foes; and you will have heard of our having triumphantly taken their Capital City of Washington, as well as many other places—beaten their armies in battle—and spread terror over the heart of their country.

Come forth, then, ye Brave Chiefs and Warriors, as one family, and join, the British Standard—the signal of union between the powerful and the oppressed—the symbol of Justice led on by Victory.

If you want covering to protect yourselves, your wives, and your children, against the winter's cold,—come to us and we will clothe you. If you want arms and ammunition to defend yourselves against your oppressors—come to us and we will provide you. Call around you the whole of our Indian brethren,—and we will show them the same token of our brotherly love.

And what think you we ask in return for this bounty of our Great Father, which we his chosen Warriors have so much pleasure in offering to you? Nothing more than that you should assist us manfully in regaining your lost lands,—the lands of your forefathers,—from the common enemy, the wicked People of the United States; and that you should hand down those lands to your children hereafter, as we hope we shall now be able to deliver them up to you, their lawful owners. And you may rest assured, that whenever we have forced our Enemies to ask for a Peace, our good Father will on no account forget the welfare of his much-loved Indian children.

Again then, brave Chiefs and Warriors of the Indian Nations, at the mandate of the Great Spirit we call upon you to come forth arrayed in battle, to fight the great fight of Justice, and recover your long-lost freedom. Animate your hearts in this sacred cause,—unite with us as the sons of our common Father,—and a great and glorious victory will shortly crown our exertions.

Given under our Hands and Seals, on Board His Britannic Majesty's Ship Tonnant, off Appalachicola, the 5ᵗʰ of December, 1814.

ALEXANDER COCHRANE
Vice-Admiral and Commander in Chief of the Fleet on the North American and Jamaica Stations.

JOHN KEANE
Major-General, Commanding the Forces

Courtesy of the University of West Florida, Special Collections.

9. General Andrew Jackson to Secretary of State James Monroe

Following the Battle of New Orleans

Camp 4 Miles Below New Orleans, January 9, 1815.

Sir:

During the days of the 6th and 7th, the enemy had been actively employed in making preparations for an attack on my lines. With infinite labor they had succeeded on the night of the 7th in getting their boats across from the lake to the river, by widening and deepening the canal on which they had effected their disembarkation. It had not been in my power to impede these operations by a general attack: added to other reasons, the nature of the troops under my command, mostly militia, rendered it too hazardous to attempt extensive offensive movements in an open country, against a numerous and well disciplined army. Although my forces, as to number, had been increased by the arrival of the Kentucky division, my strength had received very little addition; a small portion only of that detachment being provided with arms. Compelled thus to wait the attack of the enemy, I took every measure to repel it when it should be made, and to defeat the object he had in view. General Morgan, with the New Orleans contingent, the Louisiana militia and a strong detachment of the Kentucky troops, occupied an entrenched camp on the opposite side of the river, protected by strong batteries on the bank, erected and superintended by commodore Patterson.

In my encampment everything was ready for action, when, early on the morning of the 8th, the enemy after throwing a heavy shower of bombs and Congreve rockets, advanced their columns on my right and left, to storm my entrenchments. I cannot speak sufficiently in praise of the firmness and deliberation with which my whole line received their approach—more could not have been expected from veterans inured to war. For an hour the fire of the small arms was as incessant and severe as can be imagined. The artillery, too, directed by officers who displayed equal skill and courage, did great execution. Yet the columns of the enemy continued to advance with a firmness which reflects upon them the greatest credit. Twice the column which approached me on my left, was repulsed by the troops of General Carroll, those of General Coffee, and a division of the Kentucky militia, and twice they formed again and renewed the assault. At length, however, cut to pieces, they fled in confusion from the field, leaving it covered with their dead and wounded. The loss which the enemy sustained on this occasion, cannot be estimated at less than 1500 in killed, wounded and prisoners. Upwards of three hundred have already been delivered over for burial; and my men are still engaged in picking them up within my lines and carrying them to the point where the enemy are to receive them. This is in addition to the dead and wounded whom the enemy have been enabled to carry from the field, during and since the action, and to those who have since died of the wounds they have received. We have taken about 500 prisoners, upwards of 300 of whom are wounded, and a great part of them mortally. My loss has not exceeded, and I believe has not amounted to ten killed and as many wounded.

The entire destruction of the enemy's army was now inevitable, had it not been for an unfortunate occurrence which at this moment took place on the other side of the river. Simultaneously with his advance, upon my lines, he had thrown over in his boats a considerable force to the other side of the river. These having landed were hardy enough to advance against the works of General Morgan; and what is strange and difficult to account for, at the very moment when their entire discomfiture was looked for with a confidence approaching to certainty, the Kentucky reinforcements, ingloriously fled, drawing after them, by their example, the remainder of the forces; and thus yielding to the enemy that most fortunate position. The batteries which had rendered me, for many days, the most important service, though bravely defended, were of course now abandoned; not however, until the guns had been spiked.

This unfortunate route had totally changed the aspect of affairs. The enemy now occupied a position from which they might annoy us without hazard, and by means of which they might have been enabled to defeat, in a great measure, the effects of our success on this side of the river. It became therefore an object of the first consequence to dislodge him as soon as possible. For this object, all the means in my power, which I could with safety use, were immediately put in preparation. Perhaps, however, it was somewhat owing to another cause that I succeeded beyond my expectations, In negociating [sic] the terms of a temporary suspension of hostilities to enable the enemy to bury their dead and provide for their wounded, I had required certain propositions to be acceded to as a basis; among which was this one—that although hostilities should cease on this side the river until 12 o'clock of this day, yet it was not to be understood that they should cease on the other side; but that no reinforcements should be sent across by either army until the expiration of that day. His excellency major-general Lambert begged time to consider of these propositions until 10 o'clock of today, and in the meantime recrossed his troops. I need not tell you with how much eagreness [sic] *I immediately regained possession of the position he had thus hastily quitted.*

The enemy having concentered [sic] *his forces, may again attempt to drive me from my position by storm. Whenever he does, I have no doubt my men will act with their usual firmness, and sustain a character now become dear to them.*

I have the honor to be, with great respect,

Your obedient servant.

John Spencer Bassett, ed., *Correspondence of Andrew Jackson*, Vol. 2 (Washington, D.C., 1927), 136–38.

10. The Treaty of Fort Jackson

Articles of agreement and capitulation, made and concluded this ninth day of August, one thousand eight hundred and fourteen, between major general Andrew Jackson, on behalf of the President of the United States of America, and the chiefs, deputies, and warriors of the Creek Nation.

WHEREAS an unprovoked, inhuman, and sanguinary war, waged by the hostile Creeks against the United States, hath been repelled, prosecuted and determined, successfully, on the part of the said States, in conformity with principles of national justice and honorable warfare—And whereas consideration is due to the rectitude of proceeding dictated by instructions relating to the re-establishment of peace: Be it remembered, that prior to the conquest of that part of the Creek nation hostile to the United States, numberless aggressions had been committed against the peace, the property, and the lives of citizens of the United States, and those of the Creek nation in amity with her, at the mouth of Duck river, Fort Mimms, and elsewhere, contrary to national faith, and the regard due to an article of the treaty concluded at New-York, in the year seventeen hundred ninety, between the two nations: That the United States, previously to the perpetration of such outrages, did, in order to ensure future amity and concord between the Creek nation and the said states, in conformity with the stipulations of former treaties, fulfill, with punctuality and good faith, her engagements to the said nation: that more than two-thirds of the whole number of chiefs and warriors of the Creek nation, disregarding the genuine spirit of existing treaties, suffered themselves to be instigated to violations of their national honor, and the respect due to a part of their own nation faithful to the United States and the principles of humanity, by impostures [impostors,] denominating themselves Prophets, and by the duplicity and misrepresentation of foreign emissaries, whose governments are at war, open or understood, with the United States. Wherefore,

1st—The United States demand an equivalent for all expenses incurred in prosecuting the war to its termination, by a cession of all the territory belonging to the Creek nation within the territories of the United States, lying west, south, and south-eastwardly, of a line to be run and described by persons duly authorized and appointed by the President of the United States—Beginning at a point on the eastern bank of the Coosa river, where the south boundary line of the Cherokee nation crosses the same; running from thence down the said Coosa river with its eastern bank according to its various meanders to a point one mile above the mouth of Cedar creek, at Fort Williams, thence east two miles, thence south two miles, thence west to the eastern bank of the said Coosa river, thence down the eastern bank thereof according to its various meanders to a point opposite the upper end of the great falls, (called by the natives Woetumka,) thence east from a true meridian line to a point due north of the mouth of Ofucshee, thence south by a like meridian line to the mouth of Ofucshee on the south side of the Tallapoosa river, thence up the same, according to its various meanders, to a point where a direct course will cross the same at the distance of ten miles from the mouth thereof, thence a direct line to the mouth of Summochico creek, which empties into the Chatahouchie river on the east side thereof below the Eufaulau town, thence east from a true meridian line to a point which shall intersect the line now dividing the lands claimed by the said Creek nation from those claimed and owned by the state of Georgia: Provided, nevertheless, that where any possession of any chief or warrior of the Creek nation, who shall have been friendly to the United States during the war and taken an active part therein, shall be within the territory ceded by these articles to the United States, every such person shall be entitled to a reservation of land within the said territory of one mile square, to include his improvements as near the centre thereof as may be, which shall inure to the said chief or warrior, and his descendants, so long as he or they shall continue to occupy the same, who shall be protected by and subject to the laws of the United States; but upon the voluntary abandonment thereof, by such possessor or his descendants, the right of occupancy or possession of said lands shall devolve to the United States, and be identified with the right of property ceded hereby.

2nd—The United States will guarantee to the Creek nation, the integrity of all their territory eastwardly and northwardly of the said line to be run and described as mentioned in the first article.

3d—The United States demand, that the Creek nation abandon all communication, and cease to hold any intercourse with any British or Spanish post, garrison, or town; and that they shall not admit among them, any agent or trader, who shall not derive authority to hold commercial, or other intercourse with them, by license from the President or authorized agent of the United States.

4th—The United States demand an acknowledgment of the right to establish military posts and trading houses, and to open roads within the territory, guaranteed to the Creek nation by the second article, and a right to the free navigation of all its waters.

5th—The United States demand, that a surrender be immediately made, of all the persons and property, taken from the citizens of the United States, the friendly part of the Creek nation, the Cherokee, Chickasaw, and Choctaw nations, to the respective owners; and the United States will cause to be immediately restored to the formerly hostile Creeks, all the property taken from them since their submission, either by the United States, or by any Indian nation in amity with the United States, together with all the prisoners taken from them during the war.

6th—The United States demand the caption and surrender of all the prophets and instigators of the war, whether foreigners or natives, who have not submitted to the arms of the United States, and become parties to these articles of capitulation, if ever they shall be found within the territory guaranteed to the Creek nation by the second article.

7th—The Creek nation being reduced to extreme want, and not at present having the means of subsistence, the United States, from motives of humanity, will continue to furnish gratuitously the necessaries of life, until the crops of corn can be considered competent to yield the nation a supply, and will establish trading houses in the nation, at the discretion of the President of the United States, and at such places as he shall direct, to enable the nation, by industry and economy, to procure clothing.

8th—A permanent peace shall ensue from the date of these presents forever, between the Creek nation and the United States, and between the Creek nation and the Cherokee, Chickasaw, and Choctaw nations.

9th—If in running east from the mouth of Summochico creek, it shall so happen that the settlement of the Kennards, fall within the lines of the territory hereby ceded, then, and in that case, the line shall be run east on a true meridian to Kitchofoonee creek, thence down the middle of said creek to its junction with Flint River, immediately below the Oakmulgee town, thence up the middle of Flint river to a point due east of that at which the above line struck the Kitchofoonee creek, thence east to the old line herein before mentioned, to wit: the line dividing the lands claimed by the Creek nation, from those claimed and owned by the state of Georgia.

The parties to these presents, after due consideration, for themselves and their constituents, agree to ratify and confirm the preceding articles, and constitute them the basis of a permanent peace between the two nations; and they do hereby solemnly bind themselves, and all the parties concerned and interested, to a faithful performance of every stipulation contained therein.

In testimony whereof, they have hereunto, interchangeably, set their hands and affixed their seals, the day and date above written.

Andrew Jackson, major general commanding Seventh Military District, [L.S.]
Tustunnuggee Thlucco, speaker for the Upper Creeks, his x mark, [L.S.]
Micco Aupoegau, of Toukaubatchee, his x mark, [L.S.]
Tustunnuggee Hopoiee, speaker of the Lower Creeks, his x mark, [L.S.]
Micco Achulee, of Cowetau, his x mark, [L.S.]
William McIntosh, Jr., major of Cowetau, his x mark, [L.S.]
Tuskee Eneah, of Cussetau, his x mark, [L.S.]
Faue Emautla, of Cussetau, his x mark, [L.S.]
Toukaubatchee Tustunnuggee of Hitchetee, his x mark, [L.S.]
Noble Kinnard, of Hitchetee, his x mark, [L.S.]
Hopoiee Hutkee, of Souwagoolo, his x mark, [L.S.]
Hopoiee Hutkee, for Hopoie Yoholo, of Souwogoolo, his x mark, [L.S.]
Folappo Haujo, of Eufaulau, on Chattohochee, his x mark, [L.S.]
Pachee Haujo, of Apalachoocla, his x mark, [L.S.]
Timpoeechee Bernard, Captain of Uchees, his x mark, [L.S.]
Uchee Micco, his x mark, [L.S.]
Yoholo Micco, of Kialijee, his x mark, [L.S.]
Socoskee Emautla, of Kialijee, his x mark, [L.S.]
Choocchau Haujo, of Woccocoi, his x mark, [L.S.]
Esholoctee, of Nauchee, his x mark, [L.S.]
Stinthellis Haujo, of Abecoochee, his x mark, [L.S.]
Ocfuskee Yoholo, of Toutacaugee, his x mark, [L.S.]
John O'Kelly, of Coosa, [L.S.]
Eneah Thlucco, of Immookfau, his x mark, [L.S.]

Espokokoke Haujo, of Wewoko, his x mark, [L.S.]
Eneah Thlucco Hopoiee, of Talesee, his x mark, [L.S.]
Efau Haujo, of Puccan Tallahassee, his x mark, [L.S.]
Talessee Fixico, of Ocheobofau, his x mark, [L.S.]
Nomatlee Emautla, or Captain Issacs, of Cousoudee, his x mark, [L.S.]
Tuskegee Emautla, or John Carr, of Tuskegee, his x mark, [L.S.]
Alexander Grayson, of Hillabee, his x mark, [L.S.]
Lowee, of Ocmulgee, his x mark, [L.S.]
Nocoosee Emautla, of Chuskee Tallafau, his x mark, [L.S.]
William McIntosh, for Hopoiee Haujo, of Ooseoochee, his x mark, [L.S.]
William McIntosh, for Chehahaw Tustunnuggee, of Chehahaw, his x mark, [L.S.]
William McIntosh, for Spokokee Tustunnuggee, of Otellewhoyonnee, his x mark, [L.S.]

Done at fort Jackson, in presence of—
Charles Cassedy, acting secretary,
Benjamin Hawkins, agent for Indian affairs,
Return J. Meigs, A.C. nation,
Robert Butler, Adjutant General U.S. Army,
J.C. Warren, assistant agent for Indian affairs,
George Mayfield, Alexander Curnels, George Lovett, Public interpreters.

Charles J. Kappler, comp., ed., *Indian Treaties, 1778–1883* (New York, NY, 1972), 107–10.

Bibliographic Essay and Notes on Sources

This essay highlights much of the best scholarship written about the Creek War and the War of 1812 in the Gulf South. Ranging from firsthand accounts to recently published books and articles, it includes a listing of all sources consulted in the writing of this book and details where readers may turn for more information.

As is the case with the study of any war, an appreciation of the political, economic and cultural situation in which it took place is essential for a complete understanding. Fortunately, there is a rich selection of literature focusing on Creek society and culture during the era of the Creek War and the War of 1812. Researchers may wish to start with Michael D. Green's *The Creeks: A Critical Bibliography* (Bloomington: University of Indiana Press, 1979), which contains an extensive listing of literature about Creek culture ranging from earliest history to Creek society in the twentieth century. For an intriguing study of the complex nature of Creek society during the late eighteenth and early nineteenth centuries, in which many Creek leaders could claim as much European as Native American ancestry, see Andrew K. Frank's *Creeks and Southerners: Biculturalism on the Early American Frontier* (Lincoln: University of Nebraska Press, 2005).

There are a number of books that detail the role of the American policy of assimilation in highlighting the cultural differences between Upper and Lower Creeks and bringing about conflict. Critical to understanding American-Creek relations are the writings of Agent Benjamin Hawkins, made available in edited volumes of Thomas Foster, *The Collected Works of Benjamin Hawkins, 1796–1810* (Tuscaloosa: University of Alabama Press, 2003) and C.L. Grant, *Letters, Journals and Writings of Benjamin Hawkins* (Savannah: Beehive Press, 1980). Readers may also want to consider Florette Henri's *The Southern Indians and Benjamin Hawkins, 1796–1816* (Norman: University of Oklahoma Press, 1986). For a concise explanation of the origins of Hawkins's remarkable influence among the Creeks, see Frank L. Owsley Jr.'s "Benjamin Hawkins, The First Modern Indian Agent," *Alabama Historical Quarterly* 30 (Summer 1968): 7–14. In *Creek Country: The Creek Indians and Their World* (Chapel Hill: University of North Carolina Press, 2003),

Robbie Ethridge chronicles the era of Hawkins's tenure as agent to the Creeks. Ethridge provides an excellent overview of Creek society during the period and gives particular attention to the ways tensions in that society were accentuated by increasing American encroachment and a deteriorating economy. Similarly, Ross Hassig analyzes the divisions of Creek society in "Internal Conflict in the Creek War of 1813–1814," *Ethnohistory* 21 (Summer 1974): 251–71. Douglas Barber's short article, "Council Government and the Genesis of the Creek War," *Alabama Review* 38 (July 1985): 163–74, is useful for its concise discussion of council government as an expression of the rapid changes affecting Creek society in the era.

Regarding the economic situation of Creek society, the best study of Anglo-Creek trade in the century and a half preceding the war and its consequent role in contributing to the conflict is Kathryn E. Holland Braund's *Deerskins and Duffels: The Creek Indian Trade with Anglo-America, 1685–1815* (Lincoln: University of Nebraska Press, 1996). A groundbreaking study, Braund's work illuminates the economic developments that drastically altered Creek society and accentuated the cultural divisions in the first decades of the nineteenth century. The foremost study of a single trading firm, which by extension sheds light on trading practices and patterns of Anglo-Creek interaction in the period, is William S. Coker and Thomas D. Watson's *Indian Traders of the Southeastern Spanish Borderlands: Panton, Leslie and Company and John Forbes and Company, 1783–1847* (Pensacola: University of West Florida Press, 1986).

Of studies of the role of American settlement of the Old Southwest in bringing about the conflict, one of the best is Henry DeLeon Southerland Jr. and Jerry Elijah Brown's *The Federal Road Through Georgia, the Creek Nation and Alabama, 1806–1836* (Tuscaloosa: University of Alabama, 1989). Their work is the most in-depth account of the Federal Road and the role it played in the history of the region through which it cut before, during and after the war. An abbreviated, popularized version of some of their work can be found in Brown's "The Federal Road: Tourists in the Creek Nation," *Alabama Heritage* 22 (Fall 1991): 20–31.

There are several good sources of information on Tecumseh, his vision of a Native American confederacy that could resist American settlement and the religious underpinnings of the movement he inspired. Though published over a century and a half ago, Benjamin Drake's *Life of Tecumseh, and His Brother the Prophet: With a Historical Sketch of the Shawnee Indians* (Cincinnati: E. Morgan, 1841) remains an essential reference source on the leader. Among modern biographers, John Sugden's *Tecumseh: A Life* (New York: Henry Holt and Company, 1997) stands out for its comprehensiveness. R. David Edmunds's *Tecumseh and the Quest for Indian Leadership* (New York: Little, Brown, 1984) is also useful. Scholarship on

Tecumseh's brother, Tenskwatawa, is more limited. The most useful biography of him is Edmunds's *The Shawnee Prophet* (Lincoln: University of Nebraska Press, 1983), which highlights his often underappreciated importance in organizing Native American resistance to white settlement during the War of 1812 era. Of the studies of the religious nature of Tecumseh and Tenskwatawa's appeal to the Creeks, the most relevant to this study is Joel Martin's *Sacred Revolt: The Muskogees' Struggle for a New World* (Boston: Beacon Press, 1991). Martin places the Red Stick movement in the context of the larger religious world of the Creeks and their longstanding efforts for cultural autonomy. A shorter, popularized summary of his work can be found in "The Creek Prophetic Movement," *Alabama Heritage* 23 (Winter 1992): 4–13.

Any study of the origins and the first phases of the Creek War must start with two of the earliest books to chronicle the conflict, Henry S. Halbert and Timothy H. Ball's *The Creek War of 1813 and 1814* (Chicago: Donahue and Henneberry, 1895) and Albert James Pickett's *History of Alabama and Incidentally of Georgia and Mississippi, From the Earliest Period* (Charleston: Walker and James, 1851). Without the exhaustive work of these authors, which included conducting oral interviews and corresponding with those who lived through the conflict, our knowledge of the Creek War would be significantly diminished. As one-time residents of Clarke County, Alabama, Halbert and Ball's work displays a familiarity with the sites where the war unfolded that can be found in no other volume. Readers may also want to consult some of their other writings that deal with the subject, including Halbert's "The Creek Red Stick," in *Alabama Historical Reporter* 2 (May 1884); "Creek War Incidents," in *Alabama Historical Society Transactions, 1897–1898*, 2 (1898): 95–119; "Ensign Isaac W. Davis and Hanson's Mill," in *Gulf States Historical Magazine* 1 (September 1902): 151; "An Incident of Fort Mims," in *Alabama Historical Reporter* 2 (May 1884); and "Some Inaccuracies in Claiborne's History in Regard to Tecumseh," in *Publications of the Mississippi Historical Society* 1 (1898): 101–03, as well as Ball's *A Glance into the Great South-East; Or, Clarke County, Alabama, and Its Surroundings from 1540–1877* (Tuscaloosa: Willo Publishing Co., 1962).

Other valuable early scholarship on the period that has influenced virtually all later writers are the writings of J.F.H. Claiborne, especially his *Mississippi, As a Province, Territory and State* (Jackson: Power and Barksdale, 1880), which chronicles many of the major developments in the war, and his *Life and Times of General Sam Dale, The Mississippi Partisan* (New York: Harper and Brothers, 1860), which is still the most thorough account of the life of this remarkable figure. With these authors must be mentioned George Cary Eggleston, whose *Red Eagle and the Wars with the Creek Indians of Alabama* (New York: Dodd, Mead and Co., 1878) is among the earliest accounts of the war with specific focus on William Weatherford. Even though Eggleston embellished some of the historical record on Weatherford and played a significant role in propagating some of the enduring myths about the man, his book remains a valuable reference source for its influence on a generation of writers who chronicled the conflict.

An early state historian whose writings have been utilized by virtually all authors to write on the conflict after him is Dunbar Rowland. Especially useful are his *History of Mississippi: Heart of the South* (Chicago: S.J. Clarke, 1925); "Military History of Mississippi, 1803–1898" in *The Official and Statistical Register of the State of Mississippi, 1908* (Jackson: Mississippi Department of Archives and History, 1908); and *Official Letter Books of W.C.C. Claiborne, 1801–1816* (Jackson: State Department of Archives and History, 1917). Also useful is Eron Rowland's *Andrew Jackson's Campaign Against the British or The Mississippi Territory in the War of 1812* (Jackson: Mississippi Historical Society, 1921). Mrs. Rowland provides an overview of the war's effects on the Mississippi Territory, specifically, ranging from the beginning of the conflict through the Battle of New Orleans. Her inclusion of muster rolls of almost all Mississippi Territory–based commands to serve in the war makes the book especially valuable.

There are fortunately several excellent sources for firsthand accounts of the war. Among the best are compilations of original documents written by military officials, such as battle reports and official correspondence. Among these are John Brannan's *Official Letters of the Military and Naval Officers of the United States, During the War with Great Britain in the Years 1812, 13, 14, and 15* (Washington: Way and Gideon, 1823), and Clarence Edward Carter's edited volumes of territorial papers, *The Territorial Papers of the United States, vols. 5-6, The Territory of Mississippi, 1798–1817* (Washington, D.C.: Government Printing Office, 1937–38). For published firsthand accounts of events of the opening phases of the war, see "A Prelude to the Creek War of 1813–1814," in *The Florida Historical Quarterly* 18 (April 1940): 247–66, which contains Elizabeth Howard West's reconstruction of a letter by John Innerarity describing the visit to Pensacola by the Red Stick war party that would be attacked at Burnt Corn Creek. Jeremiah Austill's account of the "Canoe Fight" is contained in *Alabama Historical Quarterly* 6 (Spring 1944): 84–86. Margaret E. Austill's "Memories of Journeying through Creek Country and Childhood in Clarke County, 1811–1814," *Alabama Historical Quarterly* 6 (Spring 1944): 92–98, details her experiences regarding one of the Tensaw District stockades she witnessed being built and in which she lived. Also useful is Leland Lengel's "The Road to Fort Mims: Judge Harry Toulmin's Observations on the Creek War, 1811–1813," *Alabama Review* 29 (January 1976): 16–36, which is based on the personal correspondence of Toulmin. One of the best first-person perspectives of the campaigns of the Georgia militia can be found in "Journal of James A. Tait for the Year 1813," *Alabama Historical Quarterly* (Winter 1940), 431–40, edited by Peter A Brannon. This brief journal of a soldier in Floyd's army discusses the training it received prior to the campaign, the construction of several of the forts associated with it, as well as the Battles at Autossee and Calabee Creek. One of the few accounts of the events of the war by a Creek is found in George Stiggins's *Creek Indian History: A Historical Narrative of the Genealogy, Traditions and Downfall of the Ispocaoga or Creek Indian Tribe of Indians* (Birmingham: University of Alabama Press, 1989). The son of a Creek mother and a European father, Stiggins (1788–1845) assembled his narrative between 1835 and 1843 while living in Macon County, Alabama. Stiggins knew many of the principal Red Stick leaders personally and had an intimate knowledge of many key events in the war.

Among modern writers, Frank Owsley Jr.'s *Struggle for the Gulf Borderlands: The Creek War and the Battle of New Orleans 1812–1815* (Tuscaloosa: University of Alabama Press, 1981) stands out as the most concise and inclusive account of the causes and campaigns of the war. Drawn exclusively from primary sources, the comprehensive book is one of the few studies that adequately attempt to place the Creek War in the context of the broader War of 1812. *Borderlands* is by far the most useful book on the Creek War and the War of 1812 yet written. Owsley's article on the battle at Fort Mims, "The Fort Mims Massacre," in *Alabama Review* 24 (July 1971): 192–204, is among the best and most concise accounts of that conflict. Alongside his work must be placed the writings of Gregory A. Waselkov, whose numerous articles and books have provided a better understanding of not only the opening phases of the Creek War, but also the complex geographical situation and cultural dynamics that played significant roles in its development. He is currently the foremost authority on the history of the Tensaw District, which figured so prominently in the outbreak of the war, as well as the Battle of Fort Mims. Especially useful among his writings is *A Conquering Spirit: Fort Mims and the Redstick War of 1813–1814* (Tuscaloosa: University of Alabama Press, 2006). This book is the most detailed and thoroughly researched account of the opening stages of the Creek War in print today. Another excellent, though less detailed, source of information is Thomas D. Clark and John D.W. Guice's *The Old Southwest, 1795–1830: Frontiers in Conflict* (Norman: University of Oklahoma Press, 1996). A trendsetting book, it is the foremost study to explore the region of the Old Southwest in which the Creek War and the War of 1812 occurred as a distinctive geographical entity with its own unique history. Though this fast-moving book contains only two chapters specifically devoted to chronicling the Creek War, it is among the best at discussing the repercussions of the war on regional history.

Though drawn almost entirely from secondary resources, Sean Michael O'Brien's *In Bitterness and In Tears: Andrew Jackson's Destruction of the Creeks and Seminoles* (Westport: Praeger, 2003) makes good use of a wide range of scholarship on the campaigns of the Creek War, ranging from early writings on the conflict to some of the most recent works on the subject. His is one of the most detailed narratives of the first phase of the war currently available. Also useful is Benjamin W. Griffith Jr.'s *McIntosh and Weatherford: Creek Indian Leaders* (Tuscaloosa: University of Alabama Press, 1988). While the author's focus is on the lives of these two influential men, the book does contain an in-depth discussion of the origins of the war and the attack on Fort Mims and a substantial amount of information on later events. Also useful is Griffith's "Chief William McIntosh: Scottish-Indian Statesman and General," *Alabama Heritage* 17 (Summer 1990): 2–17.

Researchers should be aware that of the four major campaigns of the Creek War and the War of 1812 in the Gulf South, the campaigns of the Georgia militia are by far the least studied. There is currently no in-depth study focusing solely on these campaigns, and the great majority of sources providing an overview of the conflict give them scant attention. Among the most inclusive studies is Hugh M. Thomanson's article, "Governor Peter Early and the Creek Indian Frontier, 1813–1815," *Georgia Historical Quarterly* 45 (September 1961): 223–37.

For discussion of Andrew Jackson and his campaigns against the Creeks specifically, the best source is the work of Robert Remini, the preeminent scholar on Jackson. Volume one of his three-volume masterpiece, *Andrew Jackson, The Course of American Empire, 1767–1821* (New York: Harper and Row, 1977), details Jackson's early life through his adventures in the Creek War and the War of 1812. Remini's *Andrew Jackson and His Indian Wars* (New York: Viking, 2001) chronicles Jackson's tumultuous relationship with Native Americans and his role in ultimately removing several of the southeastern tribes from the region. For Jackson's correspondence during both the Creek War and the Gulf Coast campaigns of the War of 1812, see *Correspondence of Andrew Jackson* (Washington, D.C., 1926–35) edited by John Spencer Bassett, or *The Papers of Andrew Jackson* (Knoxville, University of Tennessee Press, 1980), edited by Harold D. Moser and Sharon McPherson, especially volumes two and three. A recent biography of Jackson by H.W. Brands, *Andrew Jackson* (New York: Doubleday, 2005) also provides a worthwhile interpretation of Jackson's life, as well as insight on the war. Brands's bibliography contains information on each publication he consulted, making it a valuable reference source for researchers. Though approaching two centuries of age, John Reid and John Eaton's early biography, *The Life of Andrew Jackson, Major General, in the Service of the United States, Comprising a History of the War in the South, from the Commencement of the Creek Campaign to the Termination of Hostilities*

Before New Orleans (Philadelphia: M. Carey and Son, 1817) remains useful. James Parton's *Life of Andrew Jackson*, 3 vols. (New York: Mason Brothers, 1861) is perhaps the first serious biography of the man. A good source of information concerning the Cherokee involvement in Jackson's campaigns can be found in *Jackson's White Plumes, An Historical and Genealogical Account of Selected Families Who Supported Andrew Jackson During the Creek Indian War of 1813–1814* (Bay Minette, AL: Lavender Publishing Company, 1995) by Charlotte Hood. Finally, a short, yet well-written account of the events leading up to and of the climatic battle of Horseshoe Bend can be found in James W. Holland's *Victory at the Horseshoe: Andrew Jackson and the Creek War* (Tuscaloosa: University of Alabama Press, 2004).

Some of the most reliable accounts of the War of 1812 in the Gulf South were published shortly after its conclusion. Perhaps the best comes from Jackson's engineer, Arsène Lacarrière Latour, author of *Historical Memoir of the War in West Florida and Louisiana in 1814–1815* (Gainesville: Historic New Orleans Collection and University Press of Florida, 1999). The book remains the beginning point for any study of the campaign for New Orleans. Latour's outstanding maps are invaluable for understanding the war in the Gulf South. George Gleig's *The Campaigns of the British Army at Washington and New Orleans Under Generals Ross, Pakenham and Lambert, in the Years 1814–1815* (London: John Murray, 1827) provides a good firsthand account of the battle from the British perspective.

Among more recent studies, Wilburt S. Brown's *The Amphibious Campaign for West Florida and Louisiana 1814–1815* (University: University of Alabama Press, 1969) stands out for its comprehensiveness. Frank L. Owsley's "Jackson's Capture of Pensacola," *Alabama Review* 19 (July 1966): 175–85, remains among the most succinct and detailed accounts of that event to be printed. Likewise, his "British and Indian Activities in Spanish West Florida during the War of 1812," *Florida Historical Quarterly* 46 (October 1967): 111–23 is among the most useful overviews of British attempts to utilize the Red Sticks who had fled there following the defeat at Horseshoe Bend as the launching point for their efforts to take New Orleans. *Sink or be Sunk, The Naval Battle in the Mississippi Sound that Preceded the Battle of New Orleans* (Waveland, MS: Annabelle Publishing, 2002) by Paul Estronza La Violette is currently the only book-length treatment of the important battle of Lake Borgne available. In *Thomas ap Catesby Jones: Commodore of Manifest Destiny* (Annapolis: U.S. Naval Institute Press, 2000), Gene A. Smith provides an excellent account of the battle and Jones's role in it.

For sources specifically about New Orleans, Robert Remini's *The Battle of New Orleans, Andrew Jackson and America's First Military Victory* (New York: Penguin Books, 1999) is easily the best single volume of the battle at Chalmette. Well-written and thoroughly researched, Remini's book is as entertaining as it is informative. Winston Groom's recent popularized version of the battle, *Patriotic Fire, Andrew Jackson and Jean Laffite at the Battle of New Orleans* (New York: Alfred A. Knopf, 2006) is worth consultation even though there are several errors in his introductory discussion of the Creek War. Other noteworthy books on New Orleans include *Blaze of Glory, The Fight for New Orleans, 1814–1815* (New York: St. Martin's Press, 1971) by Samuel Carter III; *The Siege of New Orleans* (Seattle: University of Washington Press, 1961) by Charles Brooks; and Powell A. Casey's *Louisiana at the Battle of New Orleans* (New Orleans: Battle of New Orleans 150ᵗʰ Anniversary Committee of Louisiana, 1965). Robin Reilly's *The British at the Gates: The New Orleans Campaign in the War of 1812* (New York: G.P. Putnam's Sons, 1974) provides an overall view of the war from a British point of view and places it in the context of the larger international conflicts in which Great Britain was engaged. *A British Eyewitness and the Battle of New Orleans: The Memoir of Royal Navy Admiral Robert Aitchison, 1808–1827* (New Orleans: Historic New Orleans Collection, 2004), edited by Gene Smith, provides a unique first-person perspective of the campaign for the Crescent City.

The Pirates Laffite: The Treacherous World of the Corsairs of the Gulf (Orlando: Harcourt, 2005) by William C. Davis is one of the latest of the books that focus on the life of the famous Jean Laffite. Jane Lucas de Grummond's *The Baratarians and the Battle of New Orleans* (Baton Rouge: Lousiana State University Press, 1961) provides the best account of the Baratarians' contributions at New Orleans.

For a discussion of how the War of 1812 on the Gulf Coast affected the Mobile Bay region specifically, Peter J. Hamilton's *Colonial Mobile: An Historical Study* (Cambridge, MA: Riverside Press, 1910) remains the starting point nearly a century after its publication. Also useful is William S. Coker's *The Last Battle of the War of 1812: New Orleans. No, Fort Bowyer!* (Pensacola: Perdido Bay Press, 1981) and Robert Ricketts's "The Men and Ships of the British Attack on Fort Bowyer, February 1815," *Gulf South Historical Review* 5 (Spring 1990): 7–17.

There have been numerous studies of the larger War of 1812. While these for the most part contain only the most basic of information on the Creek War and the Gulf Coast campaigns, they are useful because they help contextualize those conflicts. Among the best treatments of the War of 1812 is Donald Hickey's *War of 1812: A Forgotten Conflict* (Urbana, 1999). Recent publications include A.J. Langguth's *Union 1812: The Americans Who Fought the Second War of Independence* (New York, 2006) and Walter Borneman's *1812: The War that Forged a Nation* (New York, 2004). Despite its age, Benson J. Lossing's *Pictorial Field Book of the War of 1812* (New York: Harper and Brothers, 1868) remains a valuable resource both for its narrative and the images it contains. Robert S. Quimby's *The U.S. Army in the War of 1812: An Operational and Command Study* (East Lansing: Michigan State

University Press, 1997) contains concise and well-written summaries of all of the major campaigns of the war. Though primarily focused on the larger War of 1812, John R. Elting's *Amateurs, To Arms! A Military History of the War of 1812* (Chapel Hill: Algonquin Books of Chapel Hill, 1991) is also useful, both for information on the opening of the Creek War as well as its later phases and the campaign for New Orleans. The *Encyclopedia of the War of 1812* (Santa Barbara: ABC-Clio, 1997), edited by Jeanne T. and David S. Heidler, is an outstanding overall reference resource for the study of many of the people and places important in the war.

Serious researchers may also want to consult Ed Gilbert's *Frontier Militiaman in the War of 1812: Southwestern Frontier* (Oxford, UK: Osprey Publishing, 2008), C. Edward Skeen's *Citizen Soldiers in the War of 1812* (Lexington: University Press of Kentucky, 1999) and Rene Chartrand's *Uniforms and Equipment of the United States Forces in the War of 1812* (Youngstown, NY: Old Fort Niagara Association, 1992) for information on the arms and equipment used by U.S. forces during the war.

For further information on individual historic sites associated with most of the campaigns of the Creek War and the War of 1812, consult the *Alabamians at War Public Information Subject Files* at the Alabama Department of Archives and History. These files contain a wealth of information—ranging from monographs and copies of official reports to newspaper articles—about sites associated with the war in the state of Alabama. As most of these sites were at one time part of the Mississippi Territory, the Mississippi Department of Archives and History also contains files on several of these same sites. The archives also holds several manuscript collections of relevance that can be accessed through *The Old Natchez District: A Guide to Sources in the Manuscript Collections of the Mississippi Department of Archives and History*. Another good source for concise information on the historic sites associated with the war is the National Register of Historic Places, which has on file summaries of significance and brief bibliographical information for all its registrations. For information on Fort Mitchell specifically, see Peter A. Brannon's "Fort Mitchell References," *Alabama Historical Quarterly* 21 (1959): 3–9. The National Park Service's "Revolutionary War and War of 1812 Historic Sites Study" (www.nps.gov/history/hps/abpp/revwar/rev1812survey.htm), still in progress as of the publication of this book, also promises to be a useful reference resource.

Visit us at
www.historypress.net